a Guide to

SUNDAY WORSHIP

in The United Church of Canada

Alan Barthel
David R. Newman
Paul Scott Wilson
(editor)

The United Church Publishing House

1988

ISBN – 0-919000-38-X

Publisher: R. L. Naylor
Editor-in-Chief: Peter Gordon White
Cover Art: Rod Brant
Copy Editor: Joan Neilson
Printing: Print 637 Inc.

Table of Contents

(vi)

Preface

No matter how often we may have been involved in preparation for worship, new questions and possibilities arise. That is, of course as it should be. The worship of God is not something we do by rote. Even our familiar customs and treasured traditions are no mere repetitions. Each service of worship is a unique fusion of that which has always and everywhere been done in the Church and that which is a new spiritual experience in real time and space.

For these reasons we need conversation on liturgy that arises out of our life in The United Church of Canada, but that neither begins nor ends there.

The authors of this *Guide* have combined their individual interests and scholarship in a manner that is immediately useful for next Sunday's service; at the same time they have enlarged our understanding of why choices open up to us.

We in the United Church have respect for diversity. We also know that liturgy has evolved and is evolving. All the more reason, then, for us to attend to this energizing centre of our spiritual life and witness. When we do, the result is not constricting conformity but an inner consistency.

A *Guide* is for looking up and looking into. Those who use it that way are usually ready for more than simple confirmation of what they are presently doing. Even so, these pages may yield surprises. In your congregation, do you remain seated for the reading of the Gospel? What is your wisdom about children in worship services; what is your practice? When the offering plates are brought forward, what is truly happening, what signals does the congregation receive?

Some of the findings are graceful expressions of what is generally known among us. "The goal of preaching is to nurture faith by bringing it to understanding... taking the ancient biblical text, set in its own culture and time, and bringing it into the present day with the same kind of vitality it had for its first listeners." Others are probing, showing us the sources of certain practices, some of which may be "old" in our home congregation but relatively recent innovations in the wider church. In almost every instance we become aware that as United Church people we are, appropriately, receptive to ecumenical influences past and present.

The authors all teach at Emmanuel College, which is the United Church school in the Toronto school of Theology. Their book began with conversation and progressed to written pages that were revised, re-thought, and re-written several times. The diversity of interest and breadth of experience brought to the task will be apparent in this, a brief word about the collaborators:

ALAN BARTHEL has been a full time church musician for twenty years, ten of these in the United Church. He is jointly appointed to the first chair in Church Music in Emmanuel Theological College, Toronto, and Director of Music at St. Andrew's United Church. He is a member of the national Working Unit on Worship and Liturgy, which means he is actively engaged in providing educational events across the country. He is also working

(x)

on a book of sung psalms to accompany the three year lectionary.

DAVID R. NEWMAN, Associate Professor of Worship and Preaching at Emmanuel College, brings his experience of six years as chair of the Working Unit and continuing member of the editorial committee that is producing the new generation of services. He is the principal writer of *A Sunday Liturgy*, including the introduction and guidelines there. His work is also found in a number of the other new service books. He is author of *As Often As You Do This* (D.M.C., 1981) and *Worship as Praise and Empowerment* (Pilgrim Press, 1988). He has written numerous articles on worship in journals and periodicals.

PAUL SCOTT WILSON is Associate Professor of Homiletics at Emmanuel College. He has also recently served for a year and a half as an interim minister at First United Church, Port Credit, Ontario, and brings firsthand experience of a congregation struggling to implement changes in worship. He is worship editor for *Homiletic*, has written a book on preaching, *Imagination of the Heart: New Understandings in Preaching* (Abingdon, 1988), and a novel, *Holy Week* (Wood Lake Books, 1984). He is currently working on a book on imagination in faith and worship.

These three would be first to acknowledge that there is more to be said on every topic in their Table of Contents. Wisely, they choose to offer the people of the United Church a *Guide* as a contribution to continuing conversation about our Sunday worship.

Peter Gordon White
April, 1988

(xi)

Introduction

This guide to worship is written for anyone interested in worship in The United Church of Canada. Here we try to raise some of the questions that exist in our churches, questions that may not always have been stated but which help shape our thinking about worship. There is a wisdom in our Church and a rich history and tradition of worship. Even before the union of 1925, our founding denominations had already been actively involved in hundreds of individual church unions, particularly in the West. The union of Methodists, Presbyterians and Congregationalists in 1925 was a considerable accomplishment and united worship practices as well as church courts and laws. Considerable freedom of worship expression was provided, within certain guidelines. The broad composition of the United Church was further enriched with the union of the Canadian Evangelical United Brethren in 1967.

The United Church remains a uniting church as we move toward the end of this century. In North America and throughout the world there is now a large movement focused on worship reform. This movement involves not only our immediate familial denominations of Methodists, Congregationalists and Presbyterians, but also Lutherans, Anglicans or Episcopalians, Roman Catholics – in short all of the mainstream Christian denominations of the West. The spirit of our Church's participation in this movement is reflected in the motto on our crest, *ut omnes unum sint*, that all may be one.

Many congregations are currently becoming aware of a number of new worship resources for use in the United Church. These are put out by the Working Unit on Worship and Liturgy of the Division of Mission in Canada and reflect this ecumenical trend. In addition to dealing with the Sunday service, they deal with marriage, baptism and the renewal of baptismal faith, funerals, and forthcoming are a variety of special occasion services. These contain many new ideas about worship which may supplement the richness of our current practices.

It is difficult sometimes to strike a balance between the personal dimension of worship and the corporate. We come to cherish the familiar ways of worship. The wisdom that is present in these practices needs to be recognized and affirmed if changes are to be contemplated. Whatever wisdom there may be in the new ideas, changes need to be made with great care.

As the new services reflect, over the last twenty years numerous changes have been taking place in how we may think about worship. For some people the changes can be exciting, offering the kind of direction for which they have been longing: for instance increased congregational participation and recovery of our roots. For others, the changes represented in the new services can be disorientating, especially since the explanations that accompany them are often brief.

This book tries, therefore, to help us talk together about where we have been, to interpret some of the changes being proposed, and to suggest practical guidelines for those interested in exploring some of the new directions. At present there is no guide to Sunday worship which arises out of the history and experience of our denomination, although a number of books on worship of a more general nature are in use by United Church people.

This book is intended to be helpful to sessions, worship committees, choirs, membership classes, parents and candidates preparing for baptism, families who worship together, and anyone who wants to understand worship better or to help lead in worship. Talking about the way we worship can help us articulate and indeed discover more about what we believe. It is hoped that through conversations about Sunday worship we may all find our understanding deepened and our praise of God enriched.

One of the assumptions in this book is that worship, as the Greek root of the word "liturgy" implies, is the "work of the people". "Laos" in Greek means "the people of God" – all of the people, not lay as opposed to professional. If there has been one shift more significant than any other in our understanding of worship over the last few decades it has been a new appreciation of the laity. All of the people have a role in the actual planning of the worship service and in participating in a variety of ways.

Similarly all of the people have a role in any discussion about worship, such as might be facilitated by this book. This book, of course, is not the final answer. Rather it is a probing of some of the issues that we, the authors, believe to be important along with our opinions on them. Other opinions and interpretations are possible. Other issues of equal importance may inadvertently have been missed. In this age there are so many concerns of various groups that are important to balance in planning worship. These include rich and poor, male and female, children and adults, rural and urban, small church and large church, literate and illiterate, Western Canada and Eastern Canada, and parish and college. As authors we have tried to be aware of these concerns but acknowledge our limitations in being able to meet them all. We would welcome hearing from readers in order that our own learnings may deepen and that we may continue the conversation called forth by this book.

It is intended that the book be used as a study guide and a reference tool. Because it is intended for such a wide range of people and interests, more rather than less material has been included in each entry and readers might be encouraged to read simply those sections of most relevance to them. The book is structured on the order of service as proposed in *A Sunday Liturgy* (1984). Where possible, entries have been organized in the following way: a brief statement on the meaning of each part of the service, followed by its history, United Church practice, and current ecumenical ideas. To facilitate use of this guide as a reference tool, some points that are made in relation to one part of the service may be repeated elsewhere.

Emmanuel College
75 Queen's Park Crescent
Toronto M5S 1K7

CHAPTER 1

Worship Tradition and Preparation

In the United Church we do not have one prescribed form of worship. We may go into a worship service on Vancouver Island and discover that its format is similar to one we experienced in Newfoundland, but different from another just down the road. Those energetic and visionary people who brought together our three founding denominations wanted to respect the worship practices of each. They proceeded cautiously. After the union of Methodists, Presbyterians and Congregationalists in 1925, congregations continued to follow their original denominational guidelines for worship.

It was seven years later, in 1932, that the new church published its first "service book", *The Book of Common Order*. It spoke of both form and freedom in worship as an "ordered liberty", asserting that our worship practice "shrank from a uniformity that might quench the Spirit of God in the soul of man" (p.iii). Neither the prayers, the precise scripture readings, or the specific order of service would be dictated. Nonetheless, worship was to have a "common order" and was to proceed within certain guidelines which honoured the various traditions. The founders therefore provided two orders of service which United Churches might adopt. They called these orders "directories": they were intended to give *direction toward common order* for worship services and the form of the prayers, without dictating the prayers themselves or other aspects of the service. Common prayers could be used, they were simply not prescribed. In fact, following the directories in the new service book was a collection of prayers to be used with them. This included a selection of "prayers and thanksgivings" for the pastoral prayer and a "treasury" of occasional prayers. The intent of the directories remained constant: "first, that a worshipping congregation of the Lord's people shall be free to follow the leading of the Spirit of Christ in their midst; and, secondly, that the experience of many ages of devotion shall not be lost, but preserved, – experience that has caused certain forms of prayer to glow with light and power." (p. iii) This first service book, revised in 1950, went through several printings into the 1960s.

Already by the 1950s it was becoming clear that a new service book was needed, however. In 1958, delegates to the General Council instructed the Committee on Worship to revise the *Book of Common Order*. Ten years later General Council approved the current *Service Book* which appeared in two versions in 1969, one *For the Use of the People* (green) and the other, *For the Use of Ministers Conducting Public Worship* (blue). A third *For Use in Church Courts* was planned and finally appeared in 1980. It is currently out of print and being revised.

The Committee members took care to retain the tone and intent of the early directories. As they said in the introduction to the *Service Book* (blue), the "services in this book are for the guidance and assistance of those leading or sharing in public worship. They are not provided to enforce compliance or uniformity." Use of the word, "shall", they said, wishing to

2

be delicate, "indicates not prescription but preference." And they gave their own wording to interpret the 1932 idea of "ordered liberty": "In the United Church of Canada there are no prescribed forms of worship, except part of the ordination service. Worship in the United Church of Canada is guided by directories. This means that liberty is given to each minister to use his [or her] own words in any prayer. In a directory rubrics refer to structure and content, not language."

The role of the minister in worship was central and dominant both in the early and 1969 service books. Congregational roles were limited to hymn singing, the responsive reading of the Psalm, and the Lord's Prayer. By 1969, however, the ecumenical winds were rustling through our sanctuaries, in part caused by the tempest of Vatican II reform moving through the Roman Catholic Church. The role of the minister was beginning to shift. Worship was being emphasized by Catholics and Protestants as a corporate act, belonging to and involving the entire people, not just the clergy. Our church was one of the leaders. Thus the 1969 book boldly says the following:

> ... "liturgy" literally means "people's work". This
> indicates that the celebrant at public worship is not
> the minister but the people. The minister presides
> over the people's worship and as president has cer-
> tain parts which are peculiarly his [or hers]. But the
> worship is not his [or hers] alone. It belongs to the
> whole community of God's people. (see: 1969 "In-
> troduction")

Bold words were not enough, however. If the entire people were to experience increased ownership of the worship service, they needed help. The Committee therefore published the *Service Book For The Use Of The People* (green). For the first time our church placed in the people's hands a prayer book that would "enable them to share actively in public worship".

3

The people were encouraged to participate as much as possible, not just in hymns and psalms, but in prayers and responses throughout the service as well. This volume was initially published only by The Committee on Worship and its popular reception caused it subsequently to be published under the authority of the General Council.

Since 1969, the ecumenical winds, if anything, have been blowing more strongly, and increasingly worship reform in major denominations has been moving in a common direction. The latest "service book" (if the term may be used loosely) is in the form of a new generation of services published separately in booklet form for optional use in the United Church. These continue to encourage full participation of the people in the service. The first of this new generation of services is *A Sunday Liturgy*, published in 1984. Others have appeared since then: *The Celebration of Marriage* (1985), *Baptism and the Renewal of Baptismal Faith* (1986), and *Services for Death and Burial* (1987). Forthcoming in this series are *A Service Book for Use in Church Courts* and *A Book of Pastoral Liturgies*. Their intent is to be "faithful to theological and liturgical developments both within our denomination and beyond it." (*Marriage*, p. 4) After church use, critique and revision, these may form the basis for a new composite service book authorized by the General Council to replace that of 1969.

THE ORDER OF SERVICE

Ecumenical openness was already present in the *Book of Common Order* (1932). The authors recognized "indebtedness to the service books of the ancient and medieval Church, those of the Anglican and Lutheran Communions, and those of Scottish and American Churches". (1932 "Acknowledgements") One of the debts that can be traced back to the

4

medieval church was the first of two orders of service provided in 1932. This First Directory, as it was called, has the sermon at the end. The history of this order is interesting. It is based on the daily prayer services of the monasteries. It was adapted for morning and evening, not the Sunday service, in the Church of England and did not include a sermon. Originally it had prayers mainly at the beginning and had as its central elements "(1) the meditative recitation of the Psalms as an act of praise; [and] (2) the reading of Lessons from Holy Scripture". (p. v.) Eventually a sermon was added to the end of the service, and the governing order became: the psalms, the lessons, the prayers, and the sermon. It became the preferred service for Sunday worship in the Church of England as the practice of celebrating Holy Communion declined and was adopted by the early Methodists, Presbyterians and Congregationalists.

The second order of service, referred to as the Second Directory of 1932, had the sermon much earlier in the service and was patterned on the Lord's Supper, even if communion was not being celebrated. Its main elements were "(1) the Word of God read and preached (Lessons and Sermon); [and] (2) the Fellowship of intense and intimate Prayer." (p. v.) The latter centred on a prayer which included praise, thanksgiving, dedication, intercession, commemoration of the dead, and the Lord's Prayer.

The *Service Book* of 1969 preserved the two orders of service, although it switched priority: the second order of 1932 became the first order in 1969. In this order, its authors said, there is "a simple pattern": "The Approach to God...The Word of God...[and] The Response of the people." The reason for this structure was that "it follows closely the natural theological progression of God's initiative and [our] response. When the communion elements are present, the thanksgiving

5

prayer is the great communion prayer, but the shape of the service remains the same." (*Service Book*, blue, p. 76.) The Committee noted that the second order, originating in the morning prayer service, was "never intended to have a celebration of the Lord's supper as an integral part of [its] structure". Nor was it originally intended even for the Sunday service!

The *Service Book* represented a major shift in the United Church's understanding of worship. The celebration of the Lord's Supper now became the stated norm for worship. As the Introduction says:

"Our concern is to emphasize the unity of word and sacrament. Implicit here is acceptance of the sacrament of the Lord's supper as the basic Christian service and as such normative for Christian worship. No indication is given as to how often the sacrament of the Lord's supper should be celebrated, although it is acknowledged that the early church did so weekly." ("Introduction", blue)

Later in the same book the idea is again developed:

"Throughout most of the history of the Christian church a basic principle has governed the structure of public worship. The principle is simply that sermon and supper belong together as the full diet of public worship. Where it is not possible to celebrate the Lord's supper every week, the principle, nonetheless, governs the structure." (p. 76)

The adoption of the *Service Book* by the General Council put our church on a course toward more frequent celebration of the Lord's Supper. Further, it gave preference to an order of service that was not at that time normally practised in most of our churches. The shift came without much introduction or fanfare, however, being unaccompanied by any educational material for local congregations! In the United Church it is

6

local congregations that largely have responsibility for determining worship practice.

A Sunday Liturgy was published in 1984 as the first major publication of a new committee in the United Church. Prior to 1981 there were two worship committees on the national level which were responsible for setting standards and norms for United Church worship. The Committee on Worship belonged to General Council and had as its mandate the production of service books. The Celebration Advisory Committee acted more informally and belonged to the Division of Mission in Canada. It placed greater emphasis on educational workshops in worship. These were both disbanded and a new committee which became The Working Unit on Worship and Liturgy, under the D.M.C., was formed with a combined mandate covering service books and education for worship.

A Sunday Liturgy, as its name indicates, is a new service for use in Sunday worship. The members of the Working Unit dropped the earlier order patterned on morning prayer, taking their lead from 1969. The new booklet makes provisions for those Sundays in which Holy Communion is not celebrated but continues to regard the celebration as the weekly norm. The basic service provided therefore is the Lord's Supper or Eucharist.

The word "eucharist" appears in *A Sunday Liturgy* as a description of a full service of Word and the Lord's Supper. Eucharist means "thanksgiving" and was the designation for the Sunday service in the early church. Recovering this word may help to restore the role of thanksgiving that has sometimes been lost from Christian worship.

In *A Sunday Liturgy* a service without the Lord's Supper is regarded as a variation. Readers who do not carefully read the fine print could be excused for thinking that only one service, a communion service, is being provided, and that what is

ORDERS OF SERVICE SUGGESTED FOR REGULAR WORSHIP

Sermon at end (1932 – 1st Directory; 1969 – 2nd ['32 version given here])	Patterned on Lord's Supper (1932 – 2nd; 1969 – 1st ['69 version given here])	Lord's Supper with variation 1984 *A Sunday Liturgy*
THE INTRODUCTION	**THE APPROACH**	**GATHERING**
hymn (one option)	prelude	prelude
	processional hymn (one option)	
call to worship	scripture sentences	greeting
prayer of invocation	prayer of approach	
hymn (another option)	hymn of praise (another option)	hymn of praise
prayers of confession, supplication, Lord's Prayer (optional here)	opening prayer(s) general confession private confession litany	(act of confession optional)
	assurance of pardon doxology or hymn	act of praise
THE PSALMS (one or more, sung or read)	**THE WORD OF GOD** Prayer for Grace	**SERVICE OF THE WORD**
gloria		
THE LESSONS Old Testament or Epistle	Old Testament and/or Epistle Psalm Gloria	Old Testament Lesson Psalm Epistle Lesson

canticle/psalm/hymn New Testament	Gospel hymn Sermon ascription hymn	hymn/canticle/anthem Gospel Lesson Sermon Responses to the Word Prayers of the People
THE PRAYERS (thanksgiving, supplication, intercession, Lord's Prayer) offering & anthem (or after sermon) hymn announcements	**THE RESPONSE** announcements offering (anthem) offertory prayer	**SERVICE OF THE TABLE** the peace presenting of the gifts [variation of service without communion: prayer of thanksgiving]
THE SERMON prayer (thanksgiving for the Word)	prayers (thanksgiving, inter- cession, commemoration) Lord's Prayer	the great thanksgiving the Lord's Prayer breaking of the bread & pouring of the wine sharing of the bread & cup prayer after communion
hymn blessing	hymn commissioning blessing postlude	**SENDING FORTH** hymn blessing sending forth

being said might only apply to communion Sundays. In fact the service without communion is presented as a variant of the service with communion. The Working Unit undertook educational workshops on worship across Canada that are currently in progress.

The three orders included here give a general overview to the orders of service. Detailed commentary will be provided in later chapters.

The Historical Context of Celebrating Holy Communion

While church documents of 1969 and 1984 say that celebration of Holy Communion is normative for regular worship, care needs to be taken to avoid judging worship without this sacrament as inadequate, inappropriate or unacceptable. The contemporary service which follows the Service of the Word and the Service of the Table without Communion gives a faithful rendering of the Word and offers acceptable worship to God. A preaching service in the pattern of the full service of the Word and Table, but without communion, is known as the ante-communion service, taking place before [ante] communion. It dates back to the Geneva of John Calvin, one of the founders of Reformed worship, where it was not possible to celebrate communion more than four times a year because of a local decree. For many in our free church tradition, preaching has been experienced as setting out the full story of God's salvation.

Weekly communion, while foreign to many of us, also has historical support in our rich tradition. John Calvin saw weekly communion as essential because he understood it to be scriptural, although the members of his church did not agree. He and other reformers of the sixteenth century fought attempts to separate word and sacrament. For Calvin, the Word which met us in preaching was the same Word which met us in the sacrament. John Wesley also preferred weekly communion. The services of the early Methodist Church in North America were based on John Wesley's slight revisions of the Anglican *Book of Common Prayer* (1662), as published in his *Sunday Service of the Methodists in North America* (1784). This book was not extensively used as Methodists quickly reverted to a service without communion, largely because of a lack of ordained ministers.

Weekly communion recovers the practice of the early Christian church. The service of the table is the most characteristic form of Christian worship, because it is so deeply rooted in Jesus' own ministry. We think most immediately of the Upper Room, but may also recall the many meals that are recorded, including those shared with his followers and friends, with publicans and sinners, the feeding of the five thousand, and, after his resurrection, at Emmaus (Luke 24:13-35) and in Galilee (John 21:4-14). Moreover, Jesus pictured God's coming reign as a great feast (Matthew 22:1-14). When the early Christians gathered on the Sunday to celebrate the Resurrection, having worshipped on the Jewish Sabbath in the synagogue the day before, they gathered for a meal in Jesus' name, celebrating his presence with them and looking forward to his second coming. The New Testament speaks of this practice simply as "breaking bread" (Acts 2:42, 46; 20:7).

It was not long, however, before the early Christians combined a service of scriptures, which they adapted from the synagogue, and the service of the table, to form the Sunday service. They called this service the "eucharist", being the Greek word for "thanksgiving". The two services as one unity became the distinctive form of Christian worship. This unity was already the norm by the time of Justin, a Christian lay person writing in Rome around 150 AD. He describes what Christians did when they gathered on Sunday mornings:

On the day which is called Sunday, all who live in the cities or countryside gather together in one place. And the memoirs of the apostles or the writings of the prophets are read as long as there is time. Then, when the reader has finished, the president, in a discourse, admonishes and invites the people to practise these examples of virtue. Then we all stand up together and offer prayers. And, as we mentioned before, when we have finished the prayer, bread is presented, and wine with water; the President likewise offers up prayers and thanksgivings, according to his ability, and the people assent by saying amen. The elements which have been 'eucharistized' are distributed and received by each one; and they are sent to the absent by the deacons. ("First Apology" in Bard Thomson, *Liturgies of the Western Church*, Meridian, p. 9.)

It may be noted that Justin is describing an act of worship in which all of the people have an active role to play: the readers, the president, the deacon, the people standing for different parts, offering their prayers, verbally responding, singing, and receiving the elements. What Justin is describing is a service of worship that in all of its basics is being recovered by new services today.

Not everyone is persuaded that early church practice needs to influence how we worship today. Among the things that may be said in its favour is that early church worship is common to all denominations and thus it can be one route toward greater unity among Christians. The current worship statements of the Methodists, Presbyterians, and Congregationalists in England and the United States (not to mention other major denominations) each regard communion every Sunday and increased lav participation in the services as desirable goals.

PREPARATION FOR WORSHIP

How we prepare for worship of course varies a great deal. Some of the preparation is inevitably last minute, for instance when a reader is sick or someone could not be reached. But most preparation begins early in the week, often with those involved in the service looking at the lessons, discussing the theme, choosing the hymns and so forth. Preparation may also occur in the education program of the church throughout the week or on Sunday before the service. That it also occurs at home is at least as old as the practice of shining the shoes on Saturday night. Some churches make a practice of publishing the lessons for the upcoming Sunday. Other churches make the bulletins available the day before. Individuals and families can prepare by reading the lessons, singing the hymns or by teaching responses to the younger ones over breakfast. Some of the preparation for worship may take place in the sanctuary itself. This can involve a time of prayer, of watching and hearing the people assemble, of reading the words for the service, the hymns or the scriptures, of meditating on art work, the stained glass windows, and the central symbols of the worship space, and of silence and listening to the music.

Planners and leaders of worship have additional preparations which vary from church to church. Some possibilities might simply be listed here. These include:

– Coordinating, rehearsing and timing the various roles in the service, checking movement and determining locations for individual participants and leaders to stand (this gains particular urgency in large congregations or when the sacrament of baptism or communion is being celebrated). Some congregations set goals that the service flows smoothly, has dignity, and is careful in its stewardship of time.

– Choosing worship leaders who are representative of the

congregation, paying particular attention to age, sex, and race, and rehearsing them. In addition some leaders find it important to have time alone and together to prepare, and to double-check on who will be doing what.

– Preparing the place of worship: hymn numbers, flowers, lighting candles, selecting pulpit and table cloths (antependia) of a colour appropriate to the Christian season, banners or other art work, distribution of hymn books, water glasses for the worship leaders, and if there is a microphone system, checking it for volume and tone.

– Ensuring that all people and particularly strangers will be welcomed by the ushers and by the bulletin. Being an usher is an important ministry and requires particular gifts: often an usher is the first person to meet a stranger or to recognize a person in need. The usher's job may continue in introducing strangers following the service.

– Rehearsing with the congregation any aspect of the service which might be out of the ordinary can be appropriate just prior to the service. This is also a possible place for the Announcements and could include an informal welcoming of the congregation. Guest worship leaders might be introduced. The rehearsal or announcements in this location need a definite ending and may be concluded with a clear statement by the leader: "Now let us prepare in silence for worship."

– Another possibility is that the time before the service can be used by the presider to mingle with the congregation.

– There are also formal ways of preparing for worship. In the Presbyterian and Congregational churches, the Bible often was ceremonially brought in to the pulpit or lectern by a layperson before the service began. Whatever happens before the worship begins, a time of silence allows attention to be focused.

CHAPTER 2

The Gathering

It is Sunday morning. Around us are gathered people we know so well and others we may not recognize, all waiting in the light filtering through stained glass windows for the service to begin. Each person comes with different expectations and concerns. For each what happens in the next hour is important, although not all will ever be able to say why or how. Worship matters. Anyone who has had responsibility in leading worship has had occasion to ask this question, "How can the service begin so that all people are united in a common act of praise to God?" The Gathering or opening section of the service addresses this question.

The two main parts of the service are a service of the Word, including scripture reading and preaching, and a service of the Table. Whether or not communion is being celebrated, this two-fold pattern applies. The entire service is framed at the beginning by a brief Gathering rite and at the end by a brief conclusion or Sending Forth. Until the fourth or fifth century the service began simply with the readings once everyone had gathered, preceded possibly by the salutations of the leader. As churches increased in size the rituals became more formal and the gathering or entrance rite became more cumbersome.

The wider function of the Gathering is to bring the people

together for worship in God's name. The immediate function is to prepare God's people to hear God's Word. As the people assemble for worship, individuals, many of whom feel alone, have the wonderful opportunity of experiencing again that they belong to a larger identity. It is an identity we receive in baptism as a community of believers who are the Body of Christ. *All that needs to be present in the Gathering, therefore, is a greeting in the name of our Saviour, an opening hymn of praise, and a prayer.* This prayer is often in the form of a collect, a short, formal prayer that forms a transitional movement to the hearing of the Word.

The parts of the gathering have varied slightly over the years of the United Church. The writers of *The Book of Common Order* (1932) were practical. They named this section of the service (what else?), The Introduction.

The *Service Book* (1969) changed the name to The Approach. Its authors left out some things like a call to worship but included some additions and alterations: a prelude, a prayer of confession *said by all*, possibly with a litany (the kyrie), added an assurance of pardon, dropped the Lord's Prayer to the response section, and concluded with a doxology (literal meaning: praise or honour of God) or hymn of praise.

A Sunday Liturgy (1984) changed the name to the Gathering (to stress the communal nature of the act), added a dialogue greeting, made optional the use of a confession of sin at this point (confessional elements may be picked up in later prayers), and concluded with an "Act of Praise", whether this was a doxology, hymn of praise, or anthem.

THE GATHERING SECTION

1932 THE INTRODUCTION (1st Directory)	1969 THE APPROACH (1st Order)	1984 THE GATHERING
	organ prelude	prelude
	processional hymn (optional)	processional hymn (optional)
call to worship ("Let us worship God" or appropriate scripture sentences)	scripture sentences (said or sung – suggestions on pp. 76-95, blue)	greeting (dialogue)
prayer of invocation	prayer of approach (suggestions on pp. 95-105, blue)	
sung psalm or hymn	hymn of praise (if no processional)	hymn of praise
		opening prayer(s) (possibly including pp. 105-112, blue)
prayers of confession and supplication	general confession of sin *said by all* (optional)	
	private confession litany (Kyrie: see p. 78, blue. Optional)	Kyrie (optional)
	assurance of pardon	assurance of pardon (optional)
Lord's Prayer (either here or later, after the prayers of thanksgiving and intercession)		
act of praise	doxology or hymn (optional)	act of praise

PRELUDE

The notion of music prior to the service is familiar to us,
although often conversations are taking place over it as people
gather and greet their neighbours. However, we may not be

familiar with distinguishing the Prelude (meaning a "preliminary performance, action or event") from whatever additional music is played beforehand. It is best if it is short and sharp (about two minutes) and sets the tone for the service. It takes place immediately before the first spoken or sung words of the service, or, if the Announcements are made before the service, the Prelude might follow in conjunction with or instead of the time of silent preparation for worship. It is appropriate that conversation has ceased for it.

There are some creative possibilities for the Prelude. It might be based on one of the central hymns of the service. Visual projection might serve the meditative function of medieval stained glass windows, perhaps focusing on what is to follow. A short drama may accompany the Prelude as well, perhaps acting out a hymn theme like, "O sons and daughters" accompanied by the children singing and playing rhythm instruments.

PROCESSIONAL HYMN

A common practice in many of our churches has been to have a processional, in which the choir and leaders of the service process into the sanctuary accompanied by the singing of the first hymn. The historical origin of the processional entrance goes back to fifth century Rome where the civic officials made a processional entrance to the courts. The Church, not to be outdone, adopted the practice. Here the procession was made up only of the clergy, one of them carrying the gospel to the lectern. The practice of clergy entering with the choir did not emerge until the 19th century in the Church of England. (See: Hatchett, *Commentary on the American Prayer Book*, Seabury, 1981, p. 315-17)

Processions can make a powerful impact on a worship service. They are not needed every week and may be reserved for special occasions.

Festive processionals might include various Christian symbols as a proclamation of who we are as God's gathered community. For instance, if an elaborate procession was desired, it could be led by a cross-bearer, followed by a processional banner appropriate to the day, a lighted candle signifying Christ as the light of the world, the choir, then someone carrying the Bible in an upright position (to be placed on the pulpit or lectern where it will be read – not on the communion table) followed by readers, servers, assisting ministers and the presider. Processionals are one way of involving children, who may carry the cross, banners or the Bible. Each of those in the procession comes forward at a measured pace and equally spaced: the aim is dignity appropriate to the truth we bear, hence grace without the precision of the military. The practice has been that the presider comes at the end of the procession. Even if there is no procession, the Bible may be brought to the lectern immediately prior to the beginning of the service, as has been the practice at various times in our Congregationalist and Presbyterian traditions.

Some Sundays and festivals in the Christian year offer other possibilities for processionals, for instance a Christmas Eve candlelight service. On the first Sunday of Lent a silent procession might be used. And on occasions like Palm Sunday or a major anniversary of a church, there could be a congregational processional: for this the entire congregation gathers in one place and processes as one body to the place of worship.

GREETING

When all the participants in the service have taken their places there can be a dialogue Greeting as the first words of the presider and the people, said in a warm and lively yet natural and welcoming way. The presider's function is to give unity to the service. The Greeting, the Assurance of Pardon, the preaching and presiding at the Table, and the Benediction are customarily the presider's parts as the one who provides the common thread that runs through the service. This role becomes more significant, rather than less so, in a service with a number of people taking part.

The purpose of the service is to worship God, thus the Greeting serves as the first acknowledgement that the Lord is present. In an age in which it is customary to have casual greetings at the start of many of our social gatherings, the more formal greetings which may open the service can help to emphasize the unique nature of worship. Casual greetings such as "Good morning", may be appropriate for instance before the announcements or rehearsal when these precede the service.

The Greeting may be said by the presider from the centre of the chancel facing the people, or from the pulpit or lectern or table. Additional warmth may be provided by use of a gesture of open arms, curved toward the congregation, palms forward, as if to embrace the people within the arm's reach. In a dialogue the presider may fold his or her hands when the people are speaking.

When there is no processional the worship leader(s) and choir may choose to enter quietly and unobtrusively from the side and take their places before or during the Prelude. It is unnecessary for the congregation to stand until the presider stands to address them. In this act of mutual standing, the Greeting can have built into it an acknowledgment of each

22

other's presence. It can be a mark both of courtesy and hospitality, much in the same way that standing can be a way to acknowledge the presence of a new person in the room or, with the national anthem, as a way of paying respect to the proceedings. There are biblical precedents for this on which we need not dwell (see: Ezekiel 2:1 and Deut. 18:5) but which suggest standing as a way of acknowledgement of our various ministries. An indication for the congregation to stand may be included in the bulletin. When a presider asks the people to stand the action can be interpreted as requesting a personal honour.

The Greeting involves mutual exchange. This exchange may take place simply in the action of standing but may be appropriately accompanied with a familiar exchange of words. As with the whole of the Gathering section (in worship if not in this book!), it is brief and leads as directly as possible to God's Word.

The Greeting has taken a variety of forms in the United Church. The service may begin in different ways:

1) by appropriate scripture sentences –

The Book of Common Order (1932) says that "The Minister shall call the People to worship saying, 'Let us worship God', or words to the same effect, or he [/she] may use fitting words taken from Holy Scripture…." (p.1, rubric for the First Directory).

2) by the psalm or hymn – The Second Directory of 1932 began with a psalm (sung or read) or a hymn, with no provision for a separate greeting or call to worship.

3) or by the prelude – The 1969 *Service Book*, which has a call to worship in its first order only, says that, "The people

23

may be called to worship with the playing of a suitable prelude." (p. 78 blue)

In recent decades a Greeting or call to worship has been the common practice. Many churches since 1969 have developed a practice of dialogue between the presider and the people, often immediately following a short call to worship or scripture sentences. These are appropriately brief and formal in simple acknowledgement of one another. The scripture sentences may be said by the presider or sung by the choir as an introit, but the dialogue itself is traditionally between the presider and the people.

The Greeting, which can be called the Opening Dialogue, gives all of the congregation an opportunity to affirm their various roles in the service. Several pages of appropriate scriptural sentences and ancient greetings are in the *Service Book* (blue). *A Sunday Liturgy* and all of the new services being published by the United Church, have adopted the ancient Apostolic greeting. In this the presider says, "The grace of our Lord Jesus Christ, and the love of God, and the communion of the Holy Spirit, be with you all." The people respond by saying, "And also with you." The use of ancient words of Christian heritage can enhance our sense of worship. In faith we affirm that we are also gathered with those believers who came before us and have provided faithful witness throughout the centuries.

Greetings may vary from time to time, one advantage being that these may reflect differences in the Christian year or liturgical seasons. (A greeting in the Easter season might include hallelujah, the tradition being to refrain from saying hallelujah in Lent.) A disadvantage of varied greetings can be that they depend on the congregation being so tied to the bulletin that eye contact appropriate to a greeting is lost. When the

Greeting remains the same from week to week, the response can be learned by heart, can witness to our community with one another, and can ensure the participation of all ages.

HYMN OF PRAISE

Normally, if there is no processional hymn, the hymn of praise takes place after the Greeting. As the first act of singing it serves to unite us further. This hymn may be understood as an address to God in whose name we have been greeted and may suitably reflect the season of the Christian year. Here we focus on the attributes of God that call forth praise and thanksgiving rather than focusing on something individual in ourselves. A first hymn that is strong in both text and music and easily sung assists the people in "coming together".

Hymn numbers need not be announced if they are printed in the bulletin and/or posted on the hymnboard. Verbally announced hymns tend to interrupt the flow of the worship. The announcement of the hymn may simply be in music. With a familiar tune the entire verse does not need to be played through before the congregation joins. The introduction could be in the form of an improvisation that introduces some recognizable part of the melody and announces the spirit in which the hymn should be sung. There are two schools with regard to the pace of the introductions. One says that the pace should remain the same for this introduction and the singing. The other says 'do your own thing'. However, if the purpose is to encourage and help people to sing together, we sing best if we are left in no doubt about the pace of the hymn.

There has been much discussion about the use of the Amen in our worship. Amen in the Old Testament means loosely "So be it," or, "certainly, assuredly, truly". Jesus used it at the beginning of many of his sayings (sometimes translated "Verily" or "Truly") as a way of indicating that his words were to be trusted. When we use it, it can stand as a proclamation of our faith as well as an assent to the truth of the words.

The *Hymnary* of 1930 included amens after the hymns. *The Hymn Book* of 1971 dropped them. The amens following the hymns were adopted first by the Church of England in the 1890's. The United Church adopted this practice at the same time as the Anglicans were dropping it, in the 1930's.

In dropping it from our hymns we need not lose it from our worship. Saying the Amen is the people's way of giving assent to something that has been said on their behalf. It may be said by all after the opening prayers of the day; the Lord's Prayer; the Great Prayer of Thanksgiving; after the giving of symbols in some special services; when individuals receive the elements of communion, in response to words that have been said to them (i.e. "The body of Christ...."); and in the Blessing and Sending Forth.

OPENING PRAYER OR PRAYERS

The opening prayer brings the brief gathering section to a conclusion and leads directly into the Service of the Word. With the people remaining standing it links with the Greeting (and therefore may appropriately be said by the presider). Also, it provides a transition to the reading of scripture lessons.

It can be called the prayer of the day because it addresses God in relation to the theme of the day. It can also be called the collect. A collect is a short formal prayer which is direct and to the point, providing a strong note of praise. It is objective in tone, without being cold or remote, and might try to avoid subjectivity, particularly of a kind that might be interpreted as false (i.e. "O God, we are amazed when we..."). Traditionally it begins by referring to one of God's attributes or acts; follows with a brief, simple definite petition ("Give us grace to heed their warning..."); and then concludes with a result ("That your will may be furthered...") and a doxology (a praise of God). It helps to establish that God is the first reality in worship, not us.

When this prayer leads directly into the reading of scripture, it may serve as a Prayer for Illumination which calls upon God to make us receptive to the Word. The collect may be followed by an Act of Confession.

ACT OF CONFESSION

In many churches it is the custom to have a Confession of Sin and Assurance of Pardon as part of the Opening Prayer. This prayer, with its sequence of praise, penitence and forgiveness can become long or heavy, thereby providing a poor transition to hearing the word.

The Confession of Sin may be understood as an action with its own unity. It may include: an invitation in the form of an opening call to confess based on words assuring us of God's love and mercy; followed by a Prayer of Confession often said in unison by the people; silence for individual confession; the Kyrie ("Lord have mercy..."); an Assurance of Pardon; and a Doxology or Act of Praise. The portion that is said aloud and in unison is usually best if it is general, not imputing any specific sins to the people or isolating individual failings. Specific sins are something that comes to light through the proclaimed Word, not something of which we can assume to be fully aware as we enter worship. This prayer, therefore, may express regret for the sins of the church and the world; ask for forgiveness; and request the grace to lead a new life. In the silence that follows individual sins may be confessed. For reasons of length, the people may be seated for the prayer and stand for the act of praise.

27

A weekly prayer of confession as part of the Gathering is not necessary. Although it is appropriate to enter into God's presence in a penitential mood, it is by no means necessary always to do so. As the Psalmist says, "This is the day that the Lord has made; let us rejoice and be glad in it." Or again, "I was glad when they said to me, 'Let us go to the House of the Lord!'" (122:1) The *Service Book* (1969) in its second order made the prayer of confession optional and allowed for the possibility of a prayer of supplication instead. But confession may also take place elsewhere in the service. It may be included in the Prayers of the People, after the Sermon, and in an act of confession before the offering of the gifts and followed immediately by an exchange of Peace, as an act of mutual forgiveness and reconciliation.

In the penitential seasons of Advent and Lent, it is especially appropriate to begin the service with a confessional act. During Christmas and Easter seasons (the Sundays following these holy days) the dominant note is praise, and confession may be elsewhere in the service.

Kyrie

Kyrie is the name given to the traditional litany or responsive prayer:

> Leader – Lord, have mercy.
>
> People – Christ, have mercy.
>
> Leader – Lord, have mercy.

The Kyrie is derived from ancient Jewish liturgical formula responses. The name is an abbreviation of the Greek "Kyrie eleison" which means, "Lord have mercy." In Luke's account of the healing of the lepers, the lepers stand at a distance from Jesus and cry out, "Lord have mercy upon us." (Luke 17:12ff.)

28

It is comparable to the Aramaic "Hosanna", which means "save us now". It began appearing regularly in 4th Century Jerusalem, and spread quickly throughout the Christian church as a response to petitions of a prayer of intercession. This is an unusual prayer in that it is addressed directly to Jesus, rather than to God through Jesus Christ. It has appeared in various patterns of three-fold, six-fold and nine-fold repetition.

The Kyrie has been in each of our service books although its recital varies from congregation to congregation. The Second Directory of 1932 said that after the confession the Kyrie "shall be sung or said". Each of the orders of service in the 1969 *Service Book* provides for the saying or singing of the Kyrie, with the exception of the first which substitutes the Agnes Dei (the Latin for, "Lamb of God") based on John 1:29: "O Lamb of God, who takest away the sin of the world, have mercy upon us...." (p. 4, blue). *A Sunday Liturgy* continues the practice of a Kyrie.

The Kyrie may be sung or said. There are many musical examples some of which are found in *The Hymn Book*. As an alternative, it is possible to use specific verses of hymns that have "Lord have mercy" (ie. #487, stanza 1, "Have mercy on us God most high"; #74, stanza 1, "Forgive our sins as we forgive"). The singing can be choral, congregational, or with a soloist or cantor alternating with the people.

ASSURANCE OF PARDON

While the presider and congregation have had bowed heads during the prayer, for the Assurance of Pardon it is good to have eye contact. The presider on behalf of the whole congregation is proclaiming the forgiveness for each person that has been offered us in Christ. Words of assurance may be said by both presider and people either in unison or in dialogue.

The assurance of pardon which we offer is not conditional upon our having acted first. God's grace is always "prevenient", taking place even before our own act of will. In 1932, *The Book of Common Order* had the Assurance of Pardon only in the form of a Prayer for Pardon (pp. 4 & 9). The *Service Book* relies primarily on scriptural affirmation of God's willingness to forgive followed by a declaration that the people are forgiven. It contains a number of assurances of pardon, including one example of conditional grace: "Christ Jesus came into the world to save sinners. If we confess our sins, God is just, and may be trusted to forgive our sins and cleanse us from every kind of wrong." (p. 114) *A Sunday Liturgy* provides this possibility: "Anyone in Christ becomes a new person altogether. The past is finished and gone; everything has become fresh and new. Friends, believe the good news of the gospel."

ACT OF PRAISE

For the Act of Praise that follows the Opening Prayer(s) a doxology, hymn or anthem may be sung. Generally the words "glory" or "praise" would be part of the text. It is a place where the *Gloria* (the angel's song in Lk 2:14) may be sung (or a version of it such as Luther's "All Glory be to God on High"). Other inscriptions of praise may be taken from verses of many hymns (i.e. *The Hymn Book #* 235 v. 4; see also its doxology index). An anthem of praise may alternatively be sung.

In a special service a statement of occasion or an introduction of a guest might be made after the Act of Praise. In a Covenanting Service or Ordination/Commissioning Service, this is a time for the presentation of the candidates.

CHAPTER 3

The Service of the Word

By this point in the service, we are starting to experience again what it means to be a member of God's gathered community. Whatever troublesome issues could divide individual members present are overtaken by our common purpose to worship God. The familiar sounds of the organ and the creaking pews, the visual symbols like the pulpit, font, table and cross, the presider's and other leaders' words and our own voices raised in song, the dignity of the actions and the warmth of the prayers – have united us in God's presence. We are ready to focus on God's Word for us.

The first of the two main parts of the worship service focuses on the reading and interpretation of scripture. In the ancient Jewish synagogue the Sabbath service consisted of scripture, psalms, interpretation of the scriptures and a response to the word in the form of prayer. Jesus was attending one of these services when he read from the scriptures in Luke 4: "The Spirit of the Lord is upon me...." When the early Christians combined the synagogue service of the Word with their own service of the table on Sunday, each service remained essentially intact. Hence this section is named the Service of the Word.

It includes reading of scripture, interpreting it in preaching, and response. We may tend to think that it is only the preaching which is a proclamation of God's Word, but in fact the reading is as well. Both are actions that we do in praise and service to God. In both God speaks to us.

There is a natural movement from scripture readings to the Sermon. The readings present God's Word to us and the Sermon interprets those readings for our own situation and time. When the order of service has the scripture in the middle and the Sermon at the end, we are of the mind that this natural movement is not experienced. It can be a little like having to cross a busy highway to enjoy the other half of a park. There is so much in between that the readings are often forgotten (sometimes even by the struggling preacher!) when the time for interpretation rolls around. The scripture and the sermon can form one movement and so are best adjacent to one another in the service. Together they bring our lives into focus before God's Word and the nature of God's self and will are revealed to us.

The synagogue service in Jesus' time included the reading and preaching followed by responses from the congregation. Similarly today our Service of the Word can have its own response, quite separate from the later section of response in the Service of the Table. The Sermon has already begun to call forth this response from us concerning relevant issues in our lives. The response may take a variety of forms (including baptism, for instance) and conclude in the Prayers of the People which are essentially in dialogue with the Sermon. This prayer looks at our own situation in the light of the gospel ("good news") we have heard and expresses our concerns for world, church, local and personal needs.

There have been various names given to the Service of the Word in the United Church and these indicate some changes in our understanding. The First Directory of 1932, with the Sermon at the end, named only the individual parts of the service. But the Second Directory of 1932 referred to this section as "The Word of God". The authors of the 1969 *Service Book* retained that designation for regular worship but for the service of Holy Communion, wishing to affirm Christ's presence in both word and table, named this section, "The Word of God Proclaimed and Acknowledged" and the table section, "The Word of God Enacted". *A Sunday Liturgy* uses "Service of the Word", with the subtitle, "Proclamation of the Word and Response".

The actual ordering of this section has changed very little from the beginning of the United Church. The orders of 1932 and 1969 are almost identical. *A Sunday Liturgy* in 1984 adds responses and prayers as follows:

THE SERVICE OF THE WORD

1932 2nd Directory *1969 1st Order*	*(1984)*
Prayer for Grace (essentially functioning as a Prayer of the Day; see Gathering – *Opening Prayer/s).	Prayer for Illumination (if not in the Opening Prayers)
(Two lessons only in 1932. Optional two or three in 1969.)	(Three lessons:)
Old Testament *and/or* Epistle	Old Testament Lesson
Psalm (said or sung)	Psalm
	Epistle Lesson
	Hymn (or Canticle or Anthem)
Gospel	Gospel Lesson
Hymn	
Announcements (before or after hymn – 1932 only. Moved to next major section of the service in 1969)	
Sermon	Sermon
Ascription of Glory (1969 only)	Responses to the Word
Hymn (1969 only)	Prayers of the People

Things to note in *A Sunday Liturgy*:

1) Three readings are preferred (Old Testament, Epistle, and Gospel). This is to restore to the church a practice of reading the Old Testament that was lost in the West in the sixth century when two readings became the established norm.

2) Short congregational responses are added to each of the readings.

3) Several responses and the Prayers of the People are added to the end of the Service of the Word. The possible responses are listed as follows:

34

There may be silence and/or individual reflections on the Word, a creed, a hymn, an invitation to Christian discipleship, baptism, reaffirmations of faith, testimonies, announcements of congregational life and work, individual concerns gathered for the Prayers of the People. (p. 9)

PARTS OF THE SERVICE OF THE WORD
PRAYER FOR ILLUMINATION

The Prayer for Illumination is a prayer that asks God to open our minds and hearts in order that we may hear God speaking to us through the reading of the scriptures and sermon. If this prayer has not taken place in the opening prayers, it might take place here. In the Reformed tradition to which we belong, it is both the reading of the Word and the interpretation of it through the preaching that is understood to be the Word of God. The familiar practice in many of our churches is to have this prayer (frequently, "May the Words of my mouth and the meditations of my heart be acceptable in thy sight, O Lord, my strength, and my redeemer." Ps. 19:14) immediately prior to the sermon. It makes sense to move the Prayer for Illumination prior to the readings.

THE SCRIPTURE LESSONS

It can be a wonderful thing to hear the scriptures read well. We are capable of a child-like delight in hearing familiar stories or texts read again. When read well, each word is sounded clearly and distinctly, like notes of music, with varying emphasis and pitch and pace. The words come alive even as we listen. Our hearts and minds experience events through which God spoke in former times. Through the witnesses to these events God continues to speak to us anew today. Their words have been treasured and passed on to us by those who went before. We call ourselves a people of the Book, a people whose faith is based in hearing the Word. This is one reason why the pulpit Bible is usually large and at the heart of worship. It is our community book. The norm then is that scriptures are read, free from dramatic gestures and not memorized or dramatized. The reading of scripture and the active listening to it are essential to us. They stand as distinct parts of the service of worship.

We usually think of the scriptures in three categories: the Old Testament (the record of the law and prophets), the Gospels (the record of Jesus' life, ministry and teachings) and the Epistles (the letters of Paul and other followers of Christ). The reading of three lessons, one from each of the above categories, marks both ancient Christian and recent ecumenical practice. The traditional order builds toward the Gospel as a high point and thus is Old Testament, Epistle, Gospel. We are sometimes tempted to alter the order of the readings, forgetting that there is significance even in the order of readings! The Gospel is kept closest to the sermon because it symbolizes that we are preaching the good news of Christ. The Psalm was originally conceived as a song and therefore is normally not considered a reading in its own right. Rather, it is a response to the first reading.

Sometimes in the United Church we have read only one or two lessons. *The Book of Common Order* (1932) preserved the traditional order of the readings in its second directory, and it encouraged at least two lessons (an Old Testament and/or Epistle plus the Gospel). The *Service Book* (1969) encouraged three lessons and allowed two but when there were three it had the Psalm out of place, prior to the Gospel, instead of as a response to the first lesson.

36

The reading of three lessons and the use of a lectionary (See, Appendix: Lectionary and Calendar) helps to provide an exposure to scripture which many Christians are lacking today. All lessons that are read need not be preached: it is sufficient for some simply to be heard. Multiple readings can also help safeguard against seeking overly simple biblical solutions to today's problems.

PREPARATION FOR READING AND FOR HEARING

The reading of scripture is one of the ministries of the church. Through it God's Word is proclaimed. In order that it be heard, it is important that it be read well, just as it is important that the Sermon be adequately prepared. It is our opinion that readers should be skilled and ready to devote time to preparing the reading. A congregation might try to select just a few people as regular lay readers, chosen for their gift of reading, rather than trying to share the reading equally among the members. Children and youth can be included. It is important that there be a variety of voices: old, young, male, female – in short, that they be representative of congregational diversity.

Some large congregations have individuals who are especially trained in this regard and are given the task of training others. An important part of this training can be regular Bible study dealing with the passages for the upcoming Sunday. An excellent resource is available to assist readers with the lectionary passages. It is *Celebrating Liturgy: Workbook for Lectors and Gospel Readers* and is published annually (1987, 1988) by Liturgy Training Publications, 1800 North Hermitage Avenue W., Chicago IL 60622-1101 (312 / 486-7008). The authors, Fred A. Baumer with Stephen Wroblewski, suggest interpretations of the passages as well as words to emphasize, pauses, pace and a variety of other important concerns. The

37

ministry of readers, like that of ushers and servers, can be celebrated as distinct ministries within the community and expressed in the liturgy.

In our highly visual society our attention to the spoken word alone is diminishing. Rather than trying to compensate for this by having the congregation focus on a printed page, we might develop excellent readers who engage our listening ability. Worship is meant to engage the senses and the reading of scripture depends on both seeing and hearing what is happening. A valuable pastoral ministry to the hearing impaired can be provided with sound amplification equipment in the pews, and ensuring that microphones do not get in the way of lip reading. Signing for the deaf can be an additional help where needed.

INTRODUCING AND CONCLUDING THE READINGS

It is wonderful to hear the scriptures read well. Often we need preparation to hear them however. It would seem unnatural for someone simply to start reading, pause, and then turn elsewhere in the Bible to read something completely different and without announcement. The scripture readings each have their own unity. The introduction and conclusion given to the readings is a way of honouring them in the service. Ritualized introductions and conclusions of readings began in the medieval period. They provided direct involvement of the people in the service. This is one of the places in the United Church where we traditionally have recognized the importance of ritual.

The United Church has always provided for introductions and conclusions to the readings. A familiar pattern was set out in the 1932 *Book of Common Order*, which said:

before the first Lesson is read the Minister shall say, Let us hear the Word of God, as it is contained in such a book, such a chapter, beginning at such a verse; *and likewise at the beginning of the second Lesson; and after the latter*, The Lord bless to us the reading of his Holy Word, and to his name be glory and praise. *Or else, he [she] shall say before every Lesson*, Here beginneth such a chapter, *or* such a verse of such a chapter, of such a book, *and after every Lesson*, Here endeth the first, *or* the second Lesson, *or* the Lesson. (p. 2)

Sung responses to the Lessons were provided in 1930 in *The Hymnary* (#759) taken from the Anglican *Book of Common Prayer*. One example from this section we will see revived in 1984: "Glory be to thee, O Lord" before the Lesson and "Thanks be to Thee, O Lord", after the Old Testament or Epistle lesson. "Praise be to Thee, O Christ" was sung after the Gospel Lesson. The early United Church sometimes felt more free to draw upon the Anglican and other churches than many of us today.

The 1969 *Service Book* did not offer any suggestions for introduction or conclusion of the lessons. One practice that became popular was a modification of a 1932 suggestion. It was to say, "May God add his blessing to this reading of his Holy Word." We would suggest, however, that the blessing is in the reading of the Word in itself and is not something added to it. Another practice has been to introduce the reading with an interpretation, which may in effect reduce the act of proclamation by telling the congregation what to hear. Introductions to lessons, when necessary, need only briefly set the contexts.

Interpretation may best be left to the hearing and the preaching.

A Sunday Liturgy in 1984 continued some of the 1932 practice. But it added the possibility of a dialogue between the reader and the listener. One excellent advantage of this is that children who cannot read can easily become involved. The intent of the dialogue is to affirm that reading and listening are one mutual act. Here, as in *The Hymnary* and new services of other denominations, the gospel is acknowledged in a different way from the other readings. A traditional introduction for the Old Testament and Epistle is "A reading from...." At the conclusion of the reading the reader says, "The Word of the Lord," to which the people respond, "Thanks be to God." This traditional response (a translation of the Latin "Deo Gratias" which means "thank God") came after each of the lessons and at other points in the service including the dismissal.

The reader may introduce the Gospel lesson with: "The Gospel of Jesus Christ according to..." and the people respond, "Glory to you O Christ". In concluding the reader may say "The Gospel of Christ," and the people respond, "Praise to you O Christ." Different acknowledgement is not intended to give special value to one portion of scripture over another but rather can be a way of recognizing Christ's presence. This response, unlike the responses to the Old Testament or Epistle, is addressed directly to Christ. It is similar to the Kyrie in this regard.

The presence of Christ may be symbolized by standing for the reading of the Gospel, in the same way that we stand for the Greeting and in other acts of praise. This dates back to the late 4th century and what are known as the Apostolic Constitutions or rules of worship. (These, incidentally, also assigned the reading of the gospel to the deacons)

It is often helpful that following each reading there is a brief period of silence to enable reflection on what has been heard.

All aspects of the reading have potential to speak to people of any age: the reader's manner and gestures, the visual symbol of the Bible on the pulpit, the possible placement of a lighted candle by it to indicate that the Word is light, the dignified reading, and the time of silence.

If it is desirable to have additional readings other than Biblical texts, these may be offered in three ways:

1) as a response to a lesson (analogous to a hymn, provided that there is a direct connection to the Word),

2) as part of the text of the sermon, or

3) as part of the response to the sermon.

We might want to remember that other readings are not a substitute for the reading of the scriptures and therefore should be given less prominence.

While the norm is that scripture is read, on some special occasions a text might be memorized and told or acted out. This may be done singly, in unison, or with alternating parts, with some assigned to the congregation. When this constitutes an interpretation of the text it may be better following the reading rather than as a substitute for it. The reading can occasionally be accompanied with film, slides, dance, mime or singing.

The reading of the Scripture takes place from the location of the pulpit Bible, which is the pulpit or, in the situation of there being both a lectern and a pulpit, from the lectern. (See, Appendix: Pulpit and Lectern)

PSALM

The Psalms are a book of song and prayer within the Bible and therefore somewhat distinct from other "readings". Conceived as song (the word psalm means "song"), some of their meaning is lost when they are simply read. For most of history they have been distinct from other scripture lessons. St. Athanasius pointed to this distinction when he noted that, "whereas the rest of the service speaks to us, the psalms speak for us". (*Service Book* green, p. 45) They differ from other lessons in being "a prayer of the people." (*A Sunday Liturgy*, p. 41)

Traditionally Psalms were a part of the service in which all of the congregation spoke. The congregation responded to different verses with short repeated refrains. St. John Chrysostom advised that the response be understood as an act of covenanting with God and suggested the people "gather the refrains like pearls, to keep them forever with you, to meditate upon them, to sing them to all your friends and relatives." (cited in Lucien Deiss, *Spirit and Song of the New Liturgy*, p. 107)

The Psalms form a rich part of our worship heritage, dating back to the ancient Hebrew Temple in which they were sung in a variety of ways and places in the service. They were sung by combinations of choir, soloist and congregation. It was the Jewish practice of singing psalms that gave birth to Christian sacred music. The early church adopted the use of psalms. The practice of the psalms accompanying the lessons seems to have been a Christian development, as no evidence for this is present in the synagogue prior to the eighth century (Eric Werner, *The Sacred Bridge*, p. 131). The psalms may have been read as a scripture lesson or used responsorially with a singer leading the people who would not have had the text in front of them. But by the fourth century (*Apostolic Constitutions*) the established practice in the church was to have the psalms chanted after each of the lessons. Depending upon how this was done and the type of psalm, psalms were sometimes regarded in the Christian church as a response to the lesson and sometimes as a proclamation of the Word in itself.

The English language Protestant tradition arising out of Geneva gave to Christianity metrical psalms – psalms sung to tunes with a regular metre. Calvin was the first to give this type of hymn a formal place in worship. For nearly three hundred years the Psalms were the only hymns on the Presbyterian side of the church. The Scottish Psalter of 1650 is the best known of the many metrical paraphrases in English published before and after that date.

The United Church has a rich heritage of psalmody. The pioneer Presbyterian church in North America, practised the "lining out" of the psalms. In this, a Precentor (from the Latin "to play before", i.e. one who leads the singing) would sing a line of the psalm and the congregation would repeat it. This practice originated in 16th century England and spread to Scotland in the 17th century after the appearance of the "new" 1650 Psalter. Widespread illiteracy, as well as the shortage of books made it a desirable practice in pioneer North America. The *Hymnary* of 1930, seeking to retain "the stateliness and tenderness of the Scottish Psalter" (pp. v-vi), included an entire section of metrical psalms. The current *Hymn Book* has only a few.

Issac Watts, bored with the limitations of metrical psalms, penned such hymns as "Jesus Shall Reign Where'er the Sun", based on Psalm 72. The Methodists, Congregationalists and Evangelical United Brethren have given us many Psalm paraphrases as well as a strong tradition of enthusiastic singing. From the Anglicans (through the Methodists), we received the Anglican Chant form which some of our congregations use – many congregations which read the psalms responsively often sing the "Gloria Patri" to an Anglican chant.

Psalms may occur as hymns at any point in the service. After the first lesson, however, the common practice with the

43

psalm has usually meant active congregational participation in the form of reading or singing. The *Hymnary* provided for congregational participation in a responsive or unison reading or chant. The Psalter in the *Service Book* (green) "dramatized" the readings by assigning different portions to the congregation, choir and leaders.

It is only in this century that the reading of the psalms became a common practice in Reformed circles. The *Hymnary* made the psalms "therefore available for singing or for Concerted or Responsive reading". Its collection was not to be "regarded as superseding the use of the Psalter as a whole in the worship and life of the Church." ('Preface', p. vi.) The *Service Book* (green) provided no music, although it did say that "where it is possible, the psalms should from time to time continue to be chanted". (p.45)

The Psalm may be said in unison or responsively. Unfortunately when most congregations read in unison, the united voice sounds monotone and bored rather than expressive and energetic. For congregations interested in recovering the singing of the Psalm after the first lesson there are many possibilities. Because there is an ecumenical movement in this direction, there are many resources available to make the singing lively, warm and beautiful.*

Psalm singing can be a fine way to engage children in worship leadership; they learn the short responses (antiphons) easily and can teach and lead the congregation in psalm singing. A variety of musical accompaniment can be used as well, particularly for festive occasions: handbells, tone bells, woodwinds, brass, guitar, etc.

Some of the *styles of singing psalms* may be listed here:

*See: *A Psalm Sampler*, Westminster; *Psalms for Singing* and the *Worship Book*, Upper Room Press; the Lutheran and Catholic worship books; and *Worship Blueprints Guide to Planning for Worship Music*, Augsburg.

1) Responsorial Singing

This involves a response (refrain or antiphon) sung by the congregation at intervals during the Psalm itself. The response is usually a verse which contains a key thought. The body of the Psalm may be read or sung by a music leader (cantor) or the choir. Musicians can set their own responses to a phrase from a familiar hymn. For instance, with Psalms 146- 150, the final three "alleluias" from the hymn "All Creatures of Our God and King" work well.

2) Antiphonal Singing

This involves two groups singing alternately the same melody. The two groups might be choir and congregation, or two halves of the congregation. This type of singing often is set to one of the eight medieval "psalm tones" (or "tunes"), of which "The Song of Simeon" (#526, *The Hymn Book*) is an example. The Responsorial and Antiphonal styles may be combined if the congregation sings the response and two other groups alternate verses.

3) Direct Singing

This involves one group singing the entire psalm in hymn form or the choir singing one of the many choral settings.

HYMN, CANTICLE OR ANTHEM
(located between Epistle and Gospel)

The service can proceed directly from the Epistle to the Gospel, for purposes of a briefer service. Should this be the case it may be advantageous to have different readers in order

45

to symbolize that a different book is being read. Some United Church congregations and special gatherings have used dance in worship. Where this is accepted as an expression of worship, it can accompany hymns, or readings, or be a response to the readings.

If a HYMN is sung here it should be related thematically to the lessons. Like an anthem at this point, it can help us hear the scriptures. We could follow the Lutherans in calling this the Hymn of the Day and use it to sing a new hymn whose text is based on one of the scriptural themes. The children could prepare it either in their classes or at home and introduce it to the congregation. This could be a fine substitute for the children's time. There are a number of books of new hymns written for the lectionary which might be useful, including Tom Troeger and Carol Doran, *New Hymns for the Lectionary* (Oxford, 1986).

The singing of a hymn before the reading of the Gospel may have a precedent in the third century practice of singing psalms at this point. These would have alleluias as refrains in all seasons of the year except Advent and Lent which were penitential times.

A CANTICLE or "little song" is a scripture passage, other than a Psalm, set to music. It may be sung by the choir or the congregation. *The Hymn Book* contains a number of these in selections 519-526. Among these are the Song of Mary or Magnificat (Lk 1:39-56, "My soul doth magnify the Lord..."; also #495) and the Song of Simeon or Nunc Dimittis (Lk 2:29-32, "Lord, now lettest thou thy servant depart in peace..."). Many hymn settings of the canticles have appeared in the last few decades, such as "Tell Out My Soul", #495.

Traditionally canticles were not sung in the communion or

eucharistic service and were reserved for morning and evening prayer services.

A well chosen ANTHEM here makes a direct connection to the readings or to the season of the year. It should be chosen both for its musical excellence and its relevance to the service as a whole. The word "anthem" is derived from the word "antiphon" which means "sounding or answering back" and was responsorial.

A TIME WITH CHILDREN
(After the Gospel Reading)

The time with the children that we have in most of our churches is a time we set aside for several reasons: to honour our children, to instruct them, and sometimes to facilitate their movement to the church school. Often this is one of the few opportunities for the children to have direct contact with the minister(s) and for the congregation to have contact with the children. It is often noted that when this conversation is done well, the adults gain as much as the children.

There is a variety of locations for the time with children in the United Church. Frequently it is after the Gathering section or after one or all of the lessons. Placed after the Gospel lesson, which children should hear, this time may be closely associated with the sermon. The talk with the children may begin the act of interpreting the Word. Furthermore, their time in Church School could be regarded as a time of ongoing interpretation and response.

The ministry of children is to be upheld. Luther had the children teach the congregation new hymns, and we might do so as well. From a pastoral point of view, the time with the children can be a way of opening subsequent discussions within families on a variety of issues from a faith perspective.

Children can offer the adults a fresh interpretation of the scriptures seen through their eyes. This might be in the form of a short play or dramatic reading. For instance, the scripture lesson of the raising of Lazarus from the dead could be followed by a dramatic reading (an original composition, perhaps done by the children themselves?) of Lazarus coming out of the tomb and speaking. This could be accompanied by dance, mime, slides, or line drawings. Additional ideas may be found in *Gathering* (United Church) and in books like Richard Coleman's *Gospel Telling: the Art and Theology of Children's Sermons* (Eerdman's, 1982). Ways of linking the scripture to today will be discussed under Sermon.

The origin of a children's time is uncertain, but it is linked with Sunday School. The Sunday School movement began in the nineteenth century as a mission outreach often to those who would not receive education to help them read the bible and become good church members. The model was education, not worship, although there was a worship component with prayers, singing, and offering. The classes were for adults as well as children and were held either before or after worship. Often they were accompanied by mid-week class meetings. Two things happened over time: 1) the Sunday School time moved to coincide with worship, and 2) the Sunday School became for children only. When this happened varied from church to church, but it was already happening by church union in 1925.

The practice of having a children's time has problems. The fact that none of our service books has dealt with it indicates the discomfort various national worship committees have felt. *A Sunday Liturgy* mentions it briefly, only in the final guidelines. Comments on the eucharistic prayer intended for use with children (Prayer VII, p. 35) suggest that a fully intergenerational service with the children present throughout is

48

favoured. The problems with a children's time may be listed. Some are with the content of children's time:

1) Children are often offered moral lessons in the children's time that have little to do with the scriptures or with leading them into a life of faith.

2) The delight of congregations in the children is often interpreted by the children as people laughing *at* them.

Some problems are with having Sunday School at the same time as worship, thereby *excluding* children from congregational worship:

3) Both adults and children need education. Most of the Evangelical United Brethren Churches which joined the United Church in 1968 still have Sunday School for all ages.

4) Both adults and children need worship and both learn about and nurture faith by watching and participating. In our faith we say that we become the Body of Christ through word and sacrament, although we often exclude our children from this.

5) With children absent the service tends to become dominated by words and abstract ideas. The limitations of a word-dominated service can be as true for adults as they are for children, because all of the senses are not utilized.

6) Preaching that has been designed for an adult

gathering in the absence of children is often exclusive of children's experience, even as worship so easily can exclude any of those in our society who are disregarded, be they the poor, women, the sick, etc.

7) When children have "outgrown" church school, they are equally out of place in worship because they have not grown up fully participating in it.

There are problems with involving children in worship as well. These include:

1) the lack of tolerance for children's behaviour that some worshippers express;

2) the anxiety of parents over the behaviour of their children;

3) the changes that many congregations might have to make in their practice of worship in order to make the worship services more inclusive of children (i.e. geared to the senses as well as to the intellect – see the suggestions in various entries here as well as Appendix: Children in Worship);

4) the changes that many ministers would have to make in their preaching if children were present (see: Sermon);

5) the difficulties many congregations might encounter in having the church school run before or

after the service and in offering classes for adults as well.

The alternative to a Time with Children is not to forget about the children. Rather it is to open the entire service so that they may be included throughout. The issue of children's participation in worship, whether in a children's time or in an intergenerational service, poses an ongoing challenge and opportunity for us. The joy in life that they can have, the openness with which they often receive God's love, and the energy with which they participate are delightful gifts in which adults are privileged to share.

SERMON

For the Protestant Reformers it was insufficient to have the scripture only read. It was necessary that it be interpreted as well. The Word of God is best thought of as an "event", a "happening" or an "action". God's Word is not the words of the scriptures as they lie on the page; rather it is these words as they come to life in the lives of the congregation as they hear them with the aid of the Holy Spirit. Thus each worship service is a celebration of the Incarnation, the Word becoming flesh. The responsibility for good preaching rests with both the preacher, who brings prayer, study and time to the task, and with the hearers, who listen for God to speak through what is said. Dietrich Bonhoeffer counselled his students with good advice: each time we listen to preaching we should listen with the expectation of encountering the Risen Christ.

The preaching ministry traditionally has presumed ordination and the training for the ministry of Word and Sacrament. (It is only recently that we speak of ordination to Word, Sacrament and Pastoral Care.) In fact, universities were started by the church in order to prepare ministers for these duties. The goal of preaching is to nurture faith by bringing to it understanding. This involves taking the ancient biblical text, set in its own culture and time, and bringing it into the present day with the same kind of vitality it had for its first listeners. Individual verses find their meaning not in isolation from each other, but in the context of the other verses around them.

The authority for preaching comes from Christ's command at the end of Matthew's Gospel to make disciples of all the nations. It is Christ we preach. It is to underline this authority that the sermon traditionally follows immediately after the Gospel reading. Even as the scripture readings culminate in the reading of the Gospel, the sermon flows directly from that point to develop the good news of Christ for today. When the Gospel is not the text being preached, the order of the readings (Old Testament, Epistle, Gospel) remains the same. It is our understanding of Christ that leads us to interpret scripture the way we do.

While it is necessary that the scriptures be read *and* interpreted, it is not necessary that every lesson read be interpreted. There is merit in simply hearing the scriptures. It is sufficiently difficult to do justice to one text in the preaching time that is available.

Preaching originated in the synagogues (see: Luke 4:16ff; Acts 13:14ff) and was adopted by the early church. Paul preached at Troas before the breaking of the bread. As material for preaching, the stories about Jesus were used even before they were gathered into our gospels. Paul intended his letters to be read in the worship assembly (I Cor. 16:22-24), and they also became preaching material.

Early preaching served a variety of functions. Not all of it occurred in worship services. Some was evangelical or missionary preaching for the purpose of teaching those who were unfamiliar with Christianity (Acts 10:42). Some preaching was to nurture those already committed to Christ (e.g. The Epistle to the Hebrews). And some was to teach Christian doctrine. While preaching was not always done in the worship context, it was a part of regular worship, at least until the Middle Ages when it fell into disuse. However, during this period there were movements toward the recovery of preaching, led by great preaching orders of monks such as the Dominicans. The Protestant Reformers also sought to recapture the importance of preaching. Combined with a rejection of many of the ceremonial practices and visual elements in worship by many of the Reformers, the outcome was a service of worship that was almost entirely word-centred.

Preaching has remained a strong part of our heritage and serves many of the functions it did in the early church. In this century it has taken various forms, including: doctrinal preaching which develops Christian doctrines or teachings; expository preaching which develops a biblical text, often verse by verse; and thematic preaching which develops a particular theme or idea based in biblical understanding. Part of our free pulpit tradition is that the preacher may determine not only which text(s) to read but also the manner of the preaching. Lectionary preaching, which has emerged with new vigour in the last fifteen years, has been a means whereby preachers may broaden the texts they might normally have chosen to preach. It also assists in making the preaching biblical.

The sermon is like a tree growing over a rock with roots on two sides: it must link the meanings of the biblical text in its own day with today. Karl Barth was getting at this when he said that a preacher should have the Bible in one hand and the newspaper in the other. Contemporary experiences, experiences in the lives of the congregation and of people throughout the world, must inform what is said. It is to these experiences that we bring the light of the gospel message. One way of ensuring that this happens is to place greater emphasis on the role of story in preaching, not to exclude more doctrinal kinds of reflection, but to achieve a better balance between experience and doctrine than has often been the case in the past. This balance can help to sustain the interest of both the children, if they are present for the sermon, and the adults. As with other parts of the service, like the prayers, care must be taken to ensure that experiences of children as well as adults are part of the fabric of what is said. It is often argued that children are a distraction if they are present for the sermon. It could also be argued that with the children present, and with a sensitive preacher who includes their experiences and speaks at a level all can understand, the sermon is better.

There are many lectionary-based resources to assist preachers, including *Gathering* (United Church); *Preaching the New Common Lectionary* (Abingdon); *Proclamation* (Fortress); and *Word and Witness* (Liturgical Publications). Specific help in writing sermons, with specific assistance with using story, may be found for instance in Fred Craddock's *Preaching* (Abingdon, 1985); Don Wardlaw's *Preaching Biblically* (Westminster, 1983); and Paul Scott Wilson's *Imagination of the Heart: New Understandings in Preaching* (Abingdon, 1988).

The location of the sermon in the order of service in the United Church has been either at the end of the service or in the middle. There were various reasons the 1969 *Service Book* moved away from the sermon at the end. (See the beginning of this chapter.) Among these were that it separated the reading of scripture and the preaching, that it broke the unity of the service of the Word, and that there was no opportunity for the people to respond to the preached Word.

Preaching differs from reading. In reading we are listening to the words as they are read from the page. A sermon or homily, as the root meanings imply, is a discourse or dialogue. It is a word from the person who has read the book rather than from the book alone. It is intended to have the characteristics of a conversation: varying and expressive voice, sufficient volume for everyone, eye contact, gesture. Some of our boxed pulpits, it might be argued, tend to diminish the physical impact of the preaching by blocking the preacher's body from view, which may be one reason some preachers come out from behind the pulpit (see, Appendix: Pulpit, Table and Font).

Although preachers in our church are not required to wear gowns or vestments, the practice is widespread. One argument in favour of them is that it is the office of preacher, not the preacher as person, which is the focus during the proclamation of the Word. It is not the gown which is the mark of ordination, it is the way in which the stole is worn over the gown. Stoles are intended to be worn only with gowns (see, Appendix: Gowns/Vestments) and not over street clothes.

The length of sermons varies in our tradition from ten to thirty minutes. One result of the renewal of worship in our current age is that other parts of the service are able to carry some of what has been traditionally expected of the sermon (see, for instance, Prayer of Thanksgiving/ The Great Thanksgiving). In services in which the sermon dominates, and particularly in those orders of service in which the sermon comes at the end, if the sermon is weak the entire worship may suffer. If the service is less dominated by the sermon, that need not be the case. Other aspects of the service can be trusted to help carry the message.

Briefer sermons need not be weaker sermons. They can, in fact, be more powerful, particularly if they are well prepared. It is often harder to prepare a good short sermon than a long one. Evidence indicates that the average attention span of congregations today is twelve or thirteen minutes. The suggestion that sermons may be briefer is in no sense to diminish the importance of preaching. The spoken Word, what Luther called the *viva vox Dei* (the living word of God), is an indispensable part of the service. In the sermon we are called to faith and our faith is constantly nurtured and renewed. To speak of the sermon as the Word of God is to affirm the actual presence of Christ in the preaching as strongly as in the sacraments.

RESPONSES TO THE WORD

There are a number of responses to the Word which are appropriate to this section of the service, immediately following the Sermon.

SILENCE

Following the sermon, as after each reading, a brief time of silence may enable reflection on what has been said. The importance of silence, perhaps too often ignored in our worship, has been noted for instance by Habbakuk: "But the Lord is in his holy temple. Let all the earth keep silence before him" (Hab. 2:20) Words are not always the only way we can respond to God's word. Even our words can become icons. A time of silence allows for the Spirit to speak to us in non-verbal or preverbal ways. Just as any great musical composition is a mixture of sound and silence, so too the liturgy is a weaving of the two together.

Our worship services sometimes suggest that we are afraid of silence. With television we often speak of silence as dead time. In services we may cover up what could be silent time with music as a kind of filler, for instance when the children leave the service. Many of us have experienced how, when coming from the country to the city, the sound is often overwhelming, or contrastingly, how when we go from city to country, we have to learn how to listen again. So too in worship we may learn how to listen again. In order for silence to work, the congregation needs to be prepared for it through education.

CREED

The sermon is to some extent a risk because it is partly an individual interpretation, even though it may attempt to be representative of the community. The creed can give a kind of stability to the preaching and engage the congregation.

In the first centuries of the church's existence the long prayer said before weekly communion (known as the Eucharistic Prayer or the Great Prayer of Thanksgiving) had a credal function. It summarized the essential belief of Christians and followed the Jewish pattern of thanking God for God's great actions. There was no separate credal statement. The practice of reciting creeds, specifically the Nicene Creed, emerged out of the major doctrinal controversies of the fourth century in opposition to heresy. The Creed was not a prayer, but was for the purpose of setting people straight. Its recital did not become a general practice in Europe until the 11th Century. The Apostles' Creed originated as a statement of faith in baptism, evolving from early confessional statements such as "Jesus is Lord" made in baptismal rites. As such it is particularly appropriate as a response to the Word within a baptismal and renewal of baptism service. "A New Creed" of the United Church emerged out of a recognition that the church in every age needs to reaffirm its faith in contemporary thought forms and language. It has received considerable ecumenical recognition. It is one statement of our contemporary United Church faith, but it could be argued that it is not a

57

replacement for the classical creeds which are universal expressions of Christian faith.

The fullest contemporary affirmation of faith may be found in the eucharistic prayers. Each of these prayers could provide the basis for a study program for new Christians. The *place for recital of creeds* may be most appropriate in services in which communion is not being celebrated or in the worship activity of various church group meetings.

Some people find it difficult to say a particular classical creed because their own belief is not expressed within the language of that creed or because it is language arising out of a different world view (i.e. descent into hell). Some people will only say certain parts of a creed, those parts they believe. However, recital of creeds today is not to correct heresy but to make a corporate act of confession, "confession" here being used as a formal profession of belief linking us to all Christians past, present and future.

There are a number of musical settings of the creeds in The Hymn Book and musical settings of the United Church Creed are beginning to appear. Luther and others have metricized the Nicene creed and set it to music.

HYMN

There is a long tradition of a close link between this hymn, the sermon and the scripture lesson. Unlike the biblical hymn between the epistle and the gospel, this one might focus on commitment, picking up on the main theme of the sermon. This can be another place to use a new or less familiar hymn, provided that there has been rehearsal time prior to the service.

INVITATION TO CHRISTIAN DISCIPLESHIP/ BAPTISM AND RENEWAL OF BAPTISMAL FAITH

The invitation to Christian discipleship could include

Baptism and renewal of baptismal faith (as in confirmation, profession of faith or reaffirmation of faith).

The United Church service booklet *Baptism and Renewal of Baptismal Faith* (1986), based on *The Report on Christian Initiation* (1984), provides a baptismal service with introduction and guidelines that will not be repeated here and should be consulted. It may simply be noted that the new service booklet is based on the conviction that "baptism, whatever the age of the candidate, is the sole rite of initiation into communicant membership in the Christian community, the body of Christ." (p. 4) It includes the baptism of children and adults as well as "the renewal of baptismal faith by individuals (as in 'confirmation' or 'profession of faith') and by the congregation." (p. 4) The Service reunites the rites of Christian initiation which include baptism, confirmation, and first communion.

Baptism happens only once, of course, but the renewal of baptismal faith might happen many times. This is a relatively new idea in the United Church where we have thought of confirmation as once in a lifetime. There are many occasions in which individuals might welcome, for a variety of reasons, the opportunity to renew baptismal vows and receive the laying on of hands: adolescence, graduation, leaving home, transfer of membership, marriage, starting a family, and retirement. Entire congregations may renew their baptismal faith at an anniversary, at which time they might adopt their mission statement or renew a community covenant.

The service of baptism has its own unity. The order in the new service is as follows:

Introduction – The Presider, standing at the Baptismal Font, introduces the service with appropriate scripture or a brief dialogue (including congregational responses) in Christ's name.

Presentation of Candidates for Baptism – The candidates, parents and their sponsors gather at the Font. (Ideally they will be standing facing both the congregation and the Font). After the presentation by the sponsor(s), questions of intent are put to adult candidates and to parents.

Presentation of those Renewing their Baptismal Faith – These participants come forward now, if they have not done so already, and the procedure is as above.

Renunciation and Declaration and Congregational Profession of Faith – The Renunciation is a statement by which the participants renounce evil and turn to Christ. In the Declaration they declare their faith and accept Jesus Christ as Saviour and Lord. In the Congregational Profession of Faith, the congregation pledges support and joins in reciting the Creed.

Prayer of Thanksgiving and Pouring of Water – This prayer is a thankful rehearsal of God's saving acts with biblical references to water. In the Prayer there is again the opportunity for congregational responses. The water is poured "visibly and audibly", perhaps by a sponsor, from a pitcher into the Font. Alternatively children or other members may pour the water at this time or prior to the Introduction, above.

Action of Baptism – This includes the baptism with water using the Trinitarian formula ("in the name of the Father, and of the Son, and of the Holy Spirit"). This is still the only one ecumenically agreed upon and its use remains the official United Church position. The baptism with water may be followed by marking the forehead of the newly baptized with the sign of the cross, with or without the use of oil. Then the action of baptism concludes with a Prayer for the Spirit with a Laying on of Hands, which is the action of confirmation. A variety of other symbolic actions may take place, such as the giving of a candle lighted from the Paschal candle and the donning of a new white garment. The newly baptized may then be presented to the congregation.

Action of Renewal of Baptismal Faith (1986 only) – Those renewing their baptismal faith remember their baptism with thanks and receive the laying on of hands with a prayer for the Holy Spirit. Water may be sprinkled on them, possibly with the use of an evergreen bough, in order that they may get in touch once again with the water of their baptism.

Blessing – following which the participants return to their places.

Baptism and the renewal of baptismal faith is a time of commitment. It follows naturally from the proclamation of the

61

Word as a response to Christ's claim on our lives. In many of our churches, however, we place the sacrament of baptism early in the service before the children have departed for their classes. The reasons for this are usually twofold. First, it is important for all of us, children and adults alike, to be reminded of our baptismal vows. Second, parents of children being baptized are often concerned that the children will be very restless if the baptism follows the Sermon. Restored to what we think is its proper place, as a response to the Word, baptism can occur in the presence of the children who have returned to the sanctuary after having been in the church school.

The baptismal service always needs careful rehearsing of all the participants if it is to go smoothly with maximum visibility for the congregation. Special rehearsal care may be needed when the Font is off to one side and difficult to see, as it unfortunately is in many of our churches. Sometimes the Font can be moved with good effect to a more prominent position in the sanctuary for baptism services.

TESTIMONIES

The first part of the worship service tends to be objective (see the discussion of Opening Prayers). This part of the service may become more subjective as we become more affected by the power of the Word.

In our evangelical tradition there has been the practice of individual witnessing to faith or testimonies. There can be room within the liturgy for such spontaneous or planned responses, particularly in smaller gatherings.

In a large assembly, where worship is generally planned and formal, testimonies might need to be rehearsed. Alternatively, testimonies may be included in the sermon. In addition, some services might be planned as special services of faith witness. In the Methodist tradition these were called faith witness services and occurred on Sunday nights. These special services might vary from the usual structure, taking the form primarily of hymn-singing, witnessing and prayer.

ANNOUNCEMENTS OF CONGREGATIONAL LIFE AND WORK

As the title suggests, the announcements, when placed here, can be understood as an offering of the people's life and work. Different members of the congregation can be involved in making the announcements and can create a lively sense of people's involvement in the whole life of the congregation. Out of these announcements might also come the gathering of individual concerns for the Prayers of the People which immediately follow.

However, there is a tension if the announcements take place here. On the one hand we want the advantage of some freedom and spontaneity. On the other hand we do not want the announcements to get out of hand so as to interrupt the movement of the service or to be seen to destroy what we maintain is the unity of the Word and Table. The announcements can be representative of the congregation's life and work, without being an exhaustive recitation of them.

PRAYERS OF THE PEOPLE

The lessons and the Sermon have affected each of us in the congregation differently. We cannot know when an idea that we may hardly have heard has given new hope to someone present with cancer. Similarly what was important for us may not have been heard by a neighbour. The Prayers of the People may be understood as our response to the encounter with Christ through the proclamation of the Word. These prayers are in dialogue with the lessons and the Sermon and we think are best led by someone other than the presider, preferably a lay person or a diaconal minister, who represents the outreach ministry of the congregation. This prayer turns outward and can be the beginning of the people's exercise of pastoral care and mission in the world.

A familiar custom has been to have a Pastoral Prayer, led by the minister, instead of Prayers of the People. The introduction to the 1969 *Service Book* says that "liberty is given to each minister to use his [/her] own words in any prayer". A read prayer, for instance from a service book, was felt to lack the sincerity of a prayer that was freely composed. Thus the Pastoral Prayer often balanced a need for both formal and spontaneous prayer. There was an expectation that it would be eloquent, capturing the prayers of the ages and moving on to our own.

At its best the Pastoral Prayer has been a form of guided meditation and a time of spiritual uplift. It was often evidence of a very deep pastoral concern and showed a pastor who was deeply involved in all aspects of the people's lives. As a result the people often felt they were known as they heard their concerns expressed in this prayer. It could be a time of beauty, holiness and intimacy with God. The success of this prayer often depended on the individual abilities of the minister. The danger of the Pastoral Prayer was that it could become further preaching rather than a prayer that captured the concerns of the people.

The practice of praying after the Sermon as a response to the Word can be traced back to the second century. These prayers gradually took the form of a litany of intercession led by the deacon with the Kyrie as the people's response. Eventually the intercessions disappeared and only the Kyrie remained. The Reformers sought to restore intercessory prayer to the liturgy. The Westminster Directory of 1644, which constitutes our Presbyterian roots, had this prayer before the Sermon. Five pages were devoted to how it should function! (i.e. "to bewaile our blindnesse of minde, hardnesse of heart, unbelief, impenitency, security, luke warmnesse, barrenesse....") It moved from confession to supplication and intercession for all manner of things in lofty and elevated language (i.e. "draw near to the throne of grace, encouraging ourselfe with the possibilty of a gracious answer of our prayers"). It was often full of scriptural reference.

The Pastoral Prayer in the United Church has tended to be a mixture of different kinds of prayers.

THE PASTORAL PRAYER

1932 Directories		1969
First (before Sermon)	Second (after Sermon)	(Both orders)
praise	thanksgiving	thanksgiving
intercession (on behalf of another)	intercession	intercession
supplication (entreaty, petition)	commemoration of the dead	commemoration of the dead
	Lord's Prayer	Lord's Prayer

The Pastoral Prayer varied in length but ideally was three to five minutes.

The Prayers of the People (1984) may offer brief confession of sin and prayer for forgiveness (if there is something specific the Sermon has raised), and thanksgivings for specific blessings. But it is primarily *intercession*, with the understanding that the thanksgiving takes place in the Service of the Table which follows.

This prayer offers concerns and thanks, paying particular attention to the following categories: *the world, the universal church, the local community, those in need and the departed.* (These categories can be important for raising issues in the preaching as well!) Various aspects of the congregation's life and mission can be raised. The congregation ideally can have direct input to the prayer and be represented in both its preparation and delivery. A litany (a prayer in which short biddings or petitions are made) may be used with versicles and responses such as, "God, hear our prayer", "And in your love answer", or "We pray to the Lord", "Lord have mercy". The responses could be said or sung.

This can be the most immediate and spontaneous element of congregational involvement. Opportunity may be given for individual concerns to be offered in silence or out loud. These can be quite specific but should be brief. They may simply raise concerns without indicating what God must do. In large congregations these concerns may be written on cards that are gathered in a prayer box in the narthex, or during announcement time. A portion of these might be read out loud. In small congregations people might offer their own concerns in silence or out loud (each person perhaps ending with a versicle like, "God, hear our prayer"...). Silence is needed to wait for individual spontaneous prayers – long enough (at least a minute) to allow people to compose their thoughts. The prayers end as the leader commends them to God and the people say, "Amen". This kind of prayer often will work best if it is also being offered in church meetings, so that some members become familiar with the practice.

The person leading this prayer might stand, head bowed, at the lectern or in the centre aisle facing the front, symbolizing that the prayers are the people's own, arising out of their life and needs. On some special occasions, audio visual resources could be used to provide a meditative way of visualizing our prayer concerns.

CHAPTER 4

The Service of the Table

As we have experienced the service to this point we will have noted, in the pews, that the focus has already begun to shift. At the beginning of the Service of the Word, when the reader turned the pages of the pulpit Bible to the correct place and began to read, our focus was on God's Word to us. By the end of that section, as the Prayers of the People end, our focus has already begun to shift to how we may enact that Word in the world. The focus is now on us. In grateful response to the Word, and in an atmosphere of spontaneity, we move into The Service of the Table. At the Table we dedicate our lives to Christ and Christ's work in the world, even as Christ gave his life for us. This culminates in an act of sharing wherein we give thanks for all that God has done for us and will accomplish through us, as members of Christ's Body. *Our actions are guided by Jesus' actions at the Table, even if communion is not being celebrated.*

This section of the service was originally a separate service in itself and has its origins in Jesus' meals with his friends, with publicans and sinners, in the Upper Room when Jesus ate with the disciples for the last time, and in the Resurrection meals. The early Christians went to the synagogue on Saturday for a scripture and prayer service (our Service of the Word)

67

SERVICE OF THE TABLE

WITH THE LORD'S SUPPER	WITHOUT THE LORD'S SUPPER	WITH THE LORD'S SUPPER
1932 (1st Directory)	1932 (2nd Directory)	1969 (1st and 2nd orders – 2nd in contemporary language)
THE HOLY COMMUNION	THE FELLOWSHIP OF PRAYER	THE WORD OF GOD ENACTED
Offering and Presentation. (Bread and wine are prepared.)	Offering and Presentation	Invitation (1st order only)
Psalm or Hymn	Psalm, Hymn or Anthem	Peace (with gestures in second order)
Prayer of Intercession (For Church, Nation, all People, and Commemoration of the Dead. These could be joined with the Prayers of Consecration, below)	Prayer (Thanksgiving, Intercession, Commemoration of the dead)	Offertory (Bread and wine are brought forward.)
Reading of I Cor. 11:23-26 (the Narrative of Institution)		Hymn
Invitation (i.e. "Ye that do truly and earnestly repent of your sins....")		Offertory Prayer
General Confession (Minister and People)		

Prayer for Pardon (Minister)

Comforable Words

Prayer of Humble Access ("We do not presume to come to this thy Table, O merciful Lord, trusting in our own righteousness....")

Prayer of Consecration

Lord's Prayer

Breaking of the Bread and Lifting of Cup

Peace (said by Minister)

Communion (After which elements are covered. Anthem during Communion suggested as "O Lamb of God" [Agnus Dei]

Post-Communion Prayer(s)

Second Offering (Optional. For benevolent purposes.)

Hymn

Blessing

Lord's Prayer

Psalm or Hymn

Blessing

Prayer of Thanksgiving and Consecration

Lord's Prayer

Fraction (breaking of bread and lifting of cup)

Distribution (Communion, after which the elements are covered)

Prayer(s) of Thanksgiving and Supplication

Hymn

Commissioning

Blessing

69

SERVICE OF THE TABLE

WITHOUT THE LORD'S SUPPER 1969	WITH THE LORD'S SUPPER 1984	WITHOUT THE LORD'S SUPPER 1984
THE RESPONSE	SERVICE OF THE TABLE	SERVICE OF THE TABLE
Announcements		
	The Peace	The Peace
Offering (Anthem)	Hymn	Hymn
Presentation	Presenting of the Gifts (lives, monetary and other gifts, bread and wine)	Presenting of the Gifts (lives, monetary and other gifts)
Offertory Prayer		

Prayers of Thanksgiving and Intercession with Commemoration of the Dead

Lord's Prayer

Hymn
Commissioning
Blessing
Organ Postlude

The Great Thanksgiving or Eucharistic Prayer

The Lord's Prayer

Breaking of the Bread and Pouring of the Wine

Sharing of the Bread and Cup

Prayer After Communion

SENDING FORTH

Hymn

Blessing
Sending Forth

The Prayer of Thanksgiving (structure similiar to the Great Thanksgiving)

The Lord's Prayer

SENDING FORTH

Hymn

Blessing
Sending Forth

71

and then gathered to break bread together on Sunday. This was in response to Jesus' Upper Room commandment to "Do this in remembrance of me." The two services became unified at least by the middle of the second century, as can be found in Justin's account of the way the Christians worshipped in Rome around 150 A.D.

The full or complete Service of the Table gets its form, however, from what Jesus said and did in the Upper Room, expressed in the four verbs, "take", "bless", "break", and "give". *The Book of Common Order* of 1932 made this clear:

> The Church has always been careful to make the second movement follow (in four stages) the four verbs of the Gospel narrative: "Jesus *took* bread,...*gave thanks*,...*brake*,...*gave* to them."
> (p. vi)

From this we get our four actions: 1) the presentation of the gifts (the bread and wine being part of the gifts we offer), 2) the Great Prayer of Thanksgiving, 3) the breaking of the bread and pouring the wine, and the sharing or giving of the cup.

The orders for the Service of the Table have remained fairly consistent since 1932 with some significant changes:

A number of things may be noted:

1) In 1969 and 1984 the Narrative of Institution was returned to its traditional place within the great prayer, not before it.

2) In 1969 (2nd) and 1984 there is no Invitation to the Table at the beginning of this section of the service which adopts and moves directly to the Peace. The Invitation to the Table in 1984 comes at the point when people are being invited to the Table after the breaking of the bread and the pouring of the wine.

3) Bread and wine are brought forward with the offering in 1969 and 1984, instead of the Table being set before the service with the elements covered by a white cloth.

4) In 1984 the preferred method of communion is for the people to come forward in response to the Invitation to the Table.

PARTS OF THE SERVICE OF THE TABLE

THE PEACE

Since its introduction to the United Church in 1969, an exchange of peace has been adopted by many churches. Among early Christians a kiss of peace was a way of sealing a prayer as well as a sign of reconciliation. While in our own cultural context the Peace may not involve a kiss, it can nonetheless serve for us much of the same function of unity it did for the ancient church. It takes its place at this point in the service from Matthew 5:23-24, which says, "So if you are offering your gift at the altar, and there remember that your neighbour has something against you, leave your gift there before the altar and go; first be reconciled to your neighbour, and then come and offer your gift." (*An Inclusive Language Lectionary*, Year A) There are a number of New Testament references to a kiss of greeting, including I Peter 5:14, "Greet one another with a kiss of love. Peace to you all who belong to Christ."

As a liturgical gesture the Peace dates back at least to the second century. Justin Martyr wrote,

> At the conclusion of the prayers [of the people] we greet one another with the kiss. Then bread and a chalice containing wine mixed with water are presented to the one presiding over the brethren.

Gradually the actual gesture of the kiss itself was removed and only the words remained where the priest said to the people, "The peace of the Lord be always with you," to which the people replied, "And also with you". This was known as the *Pax* or Peace.

The first modern recovery of the exchange of Peace may have been by the Church of South India in 1962, a union similar to our own but including the Anglicans. It was followed soon after by our church in 1969 and other major denominations subsequently. In all modern liturgical revisions, some gesture appropriate to the culture is being adopted to accompany the words. The gesture might be an embrace, a handshake or mutual clasping of the hands, or a kiss as a sign of our unity in Christ. For this action it may be preferable that the people be standing so as to be able to move freely in approaching one another.

In our culture in which people rarely touch one another, any form of intimacy in worship is difficult. Some may feel uncomfortable with the invitation to exchange peace. At the same time, however, it is being increasingly recognized ecumenically that worship needs to engage all of the senses including touch as a means of celebrating creation, of pastoral care, of being present to one another and of God being present to us.

The location of the peace in the service has varied. In some cases the peace is placed after the act of confession, as an enactment of the forgiveness that has been offered. The Roman Catholic Church continues the practice, known by St. Augustine, of having the peace after the fraction and before the communion. Similarly *The Book of Common Order* in 1932, following Anglican practice, placed it (without the gestures) as the last act before the receiving of communion. The *Service Book* of 1969 restored it to its place prior to the Presenting of the Gifts.

It is important that the presider's invitation to the Peace brings out its significance for worship as unity in Christ, using words such as, "And now let us greet one another with the Peace of Christ," in order that it not become simply an invitation to say hello to the neighbour. *A Sunday Liturgy* suggests that the presider's words be, "Let us stand and greet one another with signs of love and reconciliation" or "The Peace of the Lord be with you always," to which the people respond, "And also with you." Then the people stand and exchange signs of God's Peace with an embrace or clasping of hands and words, "The peace of Christ" or simply, "Peace".

In any such spontaneous activity as this, it is important that there be some decisive way of concluding the action. This may happen with the leaders returning to their places in the chancel, by the announcement of the presentation of the gifts, or by a hymn.

To introduce the Peace to the congregation involves education. It could be done in smaller worship contexts throughout the week at meetings where some interpretation of the action is possible and people can become familiar with it.

PRESENTING OF THE GIFTS

When we present our gifts, we offer our lives at the Table, here to be transformed for the salvation of the world. The material gifts are brought forward by the people to the Table to be dedicated. The action is part of the covenant that we entered into at our baptism. The presenting of the gifts by the people has always been a part of our tradition, with the ushers bringing forward the monetary gifts. Presenting of the bread and wine is a recovery of a practice that existed before the Middle Ages but was lost in the West as the people were relegated to a more passive position in the liturgy. The Orthodox Church has retained the practice. There it is known as the Great Entrance.

Sunday services may proceed with or without the celebration of the Lord's Supper.

The offertory has been recognized not simply as a collection of money but also as a sign of the offering of the people's lives in response to the gospel. A fuller symbolizing of the offering of our lives may happen with the bringing forward of the bread and wine for the celebration of the eucharist, as was initiated in the first order of 1969. Bread and wine are the fruit of the earth and are made by the labour of human hands, as a beautiful Roman offertory prayer puts it. They are symbols of our life and work in relationship with God and the created world. In Palestine of Jesus' day bread and wine was the basic meal, the food and drink necessary for earthly existence.

Jesus *took* the bread and broke it. In keeping with this we may bring our gifts to the Table. The presentation had been called the "liturgy of the people" up to the medieval period and for it people brought not only bread and wine but also, at times, candles, oil, wheat, honey, grapes and other precious items. It was the function of the deacon to distribute these gifts in the service and after the service to the poor. The giving of *material gifts* was a direct way of showing the connection between worship and pastoral care and service in the world.

The people brought the gifts forward accompanied by music, set the Table and otherwise prepared for the eucharist (thanksgiving). As a medieval offertory hymn of St. James indicates, great importance was attached to the presentation of the gifts: "Let all mortal flesh keep silence.../Christ our God to us approacheth/ our full homage to demand." From the eleventh century, however, the presentation disappeared. From then on the service was completely taken over by the clergy and the people were relegated to the role of passive onlookers.

The importance of the offering as a dedication of our work and lives could be given greater emphasis in many services today. There are a number of problems in how the offering is commonly conducted:

1) Because of prepayment plans, the plate is often passed without contribution.

2) In some churches those who collect and present the offering are not representative of the entire congregation, old and young, male and female.

3) The collection and presentation can be either too militaristic or too casual.

4) Sometimes the plates are not put on the Table but instead are removed before the end of the service for purposes of counting. Two problems with this are:

(i) The symbolism of offering our lives is diminished when the offering is not placed on the Table.

(ii) The early departure of some members from the service to count the money belittles the importance of the remainder of the service.

5) At communion, when the Table is set before the service begins, another problem emerges: the bread and wine may not be understood as ordinary bread and wine, symbols of the work of our hands and God's. They may be understood as coming from the altar or from the clergy.

The bringing forward of material gifts can be understood to be an affirmation of the value of what the people are offering. The bread and wine may have been placed at the entrance to the church for people to see as they come in. At the presentation, one loaf of bread and one cup with a pitcher of wine, may be carried to the front, followed by the trays of small glasses and bread, if needed. These are placed on the Table in such a way as to allow the focus to remain on the one loaf and one cup. Additional loaves or vessels, as needed, can be placed on a side table (credence table) in view of the congregation.

Other gifts may also be offered at this time. The White Gift tradition we have in Advent is one instance of material offering that could be expanded. Flowers for the sick in hospital might be brought forward at this time and afterward delivered by visitation teams. Gifts for special church events or mission projects might be brought forward, to the Table or to a place nearby, to be dedicated to Christ's work.

Art may also be an offering: children's art, banners, dance or music, for instance. The anthem is an offering, not simply a background thing, even if it is being sung while the other gifts are being collected.

HYMN

The gifts may be brought forward during the singing of a hymn. If the eucharist is being celebrated, this is often known as the communion hymn. Frequently in our early practice, as the elements were uncovered, the first three verses of #220 Hymnary would be sung: "Here O my Lord I see thee face to face". After communion the last four verses were sung, beginning, "Too soon we rise, the symbols disappear...." (at which point the remaining elements would be covered). The *Service Book* recommended a hymn such as "Ye gates, lift up your heads on high." There are a number of communion hymns in the Hymn Book. For Sundays not celebrating communion the hymn might focus on offering our lives and talents and on giving thanks.

EITHER: PRAYER OF THANKSGIVING

On Sundays when the eucharist is not celebrated, a Prayer of Thanksgiving may be offered at this point, giving thanks for all that God has done for us and will accomplish through us. The gifts brought to the Table are now offered to God as part of our thanksgiving. The most complete form of this thanksgiving is the celebration of the Lord's Supper. A less complete form is simply a Prayer of Thanksgiving said from behind the Table and retaining something of the original intent of the service. A special prayer of dedication of the offering is not needed.

For those wishing guidance in composing this prayer, some of the comments about the Great Thanksgiving (see below) might be kept in mind, particularly giving thanks for all that God has done in creation, incarnation, the life and ministry of Jesus, his crucifixion and resurrection, and our hope for the final establishment of God's reign in this world. Additional

thanks and supplication might be offered for items of specific
·concern to the congregation, remembering not to duplicate the
function of the Prayers of the People. This prayer may in fact
have the form and structure of the Great Thanksgiving, including an Opening Dialogue and acclamations of the people,
without references to the bread and wine.

The tone of this Prayer of Thanksgiving is one of praise and
gratitude. It is followed by the Lord's Prayer and then by the
concluding Hymn, Blessing and Sending Forth.

OR: THE GREAT THANKSGIVING
or EUCHARISTIC PRAYER

This is the prayer said prior to communion being celebrated. It is a high point of the worship service. This second
movement of the Service of the Table, corresponds to the second of Jesus' fourfold actions ("took", *"gave thanks"*,
"broke" and "gave"). It is a most condensed yet complete
credal expression of our faith and of what it means to partake
of the body of Christ, hence there may be no need for a separate recital of a creed on these Sundays. The emphasis is on
thanksgiving (the Greek "eucharistia", eucharist) for all that
God has done.

By rehearsing in praise the story of our faith, we, as a Christian community, affirm the identity we have received in Jesus
Christ. The story we recite moves in sequence from creation
to redemption to anticipation of the fulfillment of God's will
and purpose for the world. The prayer addresses God, as the
first person of the Trinity, throughout, but speaks in the name
of Christ and calls upon the Holy Spirit. The language is both
poetic and biblical. The ordained presider leads this formal declaration of faith as the one authorized by the church to speak
on behalf of all. The congregation assents to what is said and
professes its faith by joining in the initial dialogue and

80

affirmations, and in saying or singing Amen. While we call the Great Thanksgiving a "prayer", it is not intended that people assume the usual prayer posture of bowed heads and closed eyes. The focus of the prayer is on the presider and on the bread and wine. The origins of this prayer may be found in the ancient required table prayers for Jewish meals. The Jewish blessing (*berakah*) blessed or thanked God by remembering, confessing and proclaiming God's great acts in the history of salvation, especially in the creation and covenant. Led by the head of the family, this prayer had responses recited by the family members.

The earliest Christian eucharistic prayers were said extemporaneously by the presider, probably using the praise, thanksgiving, supplication structure of the *berakah*. For the prayer, the people stood and joined in the acclamations and the Amen ("so be it") at the end. The earliest written model is given in *Apostolic Tradition* (c. 215) and is generally attributed to Hippolytus of Rome. It was not until the fourth century, however, that this prayer began to appear in a fixed form. By the time this was edited in its final form by Pope Gregory the Great (590-604), the element of thanksgiving had largely been overtaken by a penitential and sacrificial tone.

With the influx of many new Christians, often with poor understanding of the faith, church leaders came to stress the need for an appropriate attitude in approaching the Table. The result, however, was that by the Middle Ages the majority of people, feeling they were unworthy to receive the sacrament, were afraid to make their communion more than once or twice a year. Moreover, the people were encouraged to regard the sacrament as an object of devotion, kneeling in adoration of Christ during the celebration, and thus further removing the idea of both a thanksgiving and a communion meal. While originally the Prayer of Thanksgiving was spoken loudly or sung in order to be heard, in the Roman Church, from the mid-ninth century until the reforms of Vatican II in the 1960s, it was prayed only in a low voice, in a language (Latin) not understood by all, thereby excluding the people.

The Reformers sought to put an end to abuses they found in the sacrifice of the mass but they did not restore the predominance of thanksgiving in the prayer. Luther and Calvin kept part of the prayer, in particular the Narrative of Institution ("This is my body...") as the scriptural warrant for the Lord's Supper. This is why in 1932 and 1969 (3rd) the Narrative of Institution precedes the great prayer. It is only with the recent liturgical reforms of all denominations, including the Roman Catholics, that the eucharistic prayer of the early church (which includes the Narrative of Institution) has been recovered.

The specific words of the prayer may vary greatly and have in the United Church over the years. The basic parts (see below) in form, sequence (praise, thanksgiving, supplication), and mode of address have largely remained unchanged however. In *A Sunday Liturgy*, the name "great thanksgiving" or "eucharistic" prayer reclaims the emphasis in this prayer on giving thanks. *A Sunday Liturgy* contains seven eucharistic prayers, all of which reflect the ecumenical consensus that has developed around the form of the Great Thanksgiving.

The form and structure of the prayer constitute its integrity as an expression of the faith of the church. Paying attention to form and structure, an individual congregation could write its own eucharistic prayers, incorporating some of its own experience and expectations while at the same time affirming its unity with other Christians past and present.

THE STRUCTURE OF THE GREAT THANKSGIVING

1) Opening Dialogue: The earliest written model of the

prayer, attributed to Hippolytus of Rome, begins with a greeting or salutation. Based on Ruth 2:4 it calls the people to prayer: "The Lord be with you. – And also with you." This is followed by, "Lift up your hearts" (the *Sursum Corda*), from Lamentations 3:41, which was used in the Jewish *berakah* as a request to stand, the traditional posture for that blessing. The people are then invited to give thanks in words that were likely part of that same prayer: "Let us give thanks to the Lord our God". The people by their response consent to do so, "It is right to give God thanks and praise", an ancient acclamation of Greek origin. This dialogue engages the entire congregation in the prayer and through it they are enabled to join with the presider who speaks in the name of all. They continue to participate in their various responses and acclamations, culminating in the Amen at the conclusion. The opening dialogue, like the Amen, is an affirmation of the unity of all who are gathered to God through Jesus Christ. In many churches the opening dialogue is sung responsively.

2) Praise and Thanksgiving: In the Eastern liturgies this thanksgiving takes an extended story or narrative form recalling the wonders of God's creation, choosing the people of Israel, and delivering them from slavery in Egypt. Prayers in the West contained variable prefaces which changed with the day, feast, or season. (see: *A Sunday Liturgy*, Prayer I, p.15ff.) The narrative of Praise and Thanksgiving may continue after the *Sanctus* and *Benedictus* with specific focus on what God has done in Jesus Christ.

3) *Sanctus* and *Benedictus*: The *Sanctus* is an ancient hymn inspired by the song of the seraphim in Isaiah's vision in the temple (Is. 6:1-3): "Holy, holy, holy Lord,/ God of power and might,/heaven and earth are full of your glory." It was sung in the synagogue as part of the morning prayer service, and might have been used by early Christians prior to

becoming part of the eucharistic prayer, first in the East and then in the West by the mid-fifth century.

To the *Sanctus* in the mid-sixth century was joined the *Benedictus qui venit*, words of acclamation from Mt. 21:9 used to greet Jesus as he rode into Jerusalem: "Blessed is the one/ who comes in the name of the Lord./ Hosanna in the highest." This addition provides a specific reference to Christ.

The *Sanctus* and *Benedictus* may be said or sung by the entire congregation on most occasions and not just by the presider or choir: it is an act of praise that joins the people's worship with that of all Christians everywhere and at all times and with the whole company of heaven. The *Hymnary* and *The Hymn Book* have a variety of musical settings for this, none of them difficult to learn. In addition there are simple melodies based on hymn tunes like "Land of Rest" found in *Songs for a Gospel People* and "New Britain" (Amazing Grace). On some occasions the choir might sing one of the many great choral settings of the *Sanctus/Benedictus* with the text printed in the order of worship so the people can participate by reading to themselves.

Frequently the narrative of Praise and Thanksgiving continues at this point. The *Benedictus* has already begun to shift the focus to God's accomplishment of salvation in Christ. This may be continued now with stories of Jesus' life and ministry, told in a form that both adults and children can comprehend. These stories come to a climax in the Words of Institution.

4) Words of Institution or Narrative of Institution: This is simply the story of Jesus establishing the practice of the Lord's Supper: "On the night in which Jesus was betrayed, our Lord Jesus took bread...." It is a specific remembering of what Jesus did in his last meal with the disciples in the Upper Room. This essential part of the eucharistic prayer is concerned

with scriptural tradition but does not attempt literal exactness. In the medieval Roman tradition the words, "This is my body...," became the moment of consecration. The Protestant Reformers placed the emphasis on "This do in remembrance of me." In the present recovery of the full eucharistic prayer, no special moment of consecration is retained.

5) The Anamnesis and Memorial Acclamation: "Anamnesis" means "making memory" or "not forgetting", the opposite of amnesia. It is a concept inherited from the Jewish faith. We engage in "making memory" of who we are as God's people and what our purpose is. Specifically we remember Christ's passion (suffering), resurrection and ascension, and look forward to his future coming in glory. This is more than a simple act of memory or expectation, however. In remembering and doing what Jesus did, Christ's death, resurrection, and coming again are experienced as a present reality. Memory and hope bring past and future together in the present.

The Memorial Acclamation is an affirmation of this truth on the part of the congregation. It either follows or precedes the Anamnesis and might use these words: "Christ has died./ Christ is risen./ Christ will come again," OR "Dying you destroyed our death;/ rising you restored our life;/ Lord Jesus, come in glory." These take the form of a proclamation of faith or hope. Occasionally the Anamnesis and Memorial Acclamation are combined: "We remember his death,/ We proclaim his resurrection,/ We await his coming in glory."

For reasons of integrity, balance and continuity, the musical settings of the *sanctus*, memorial acclamation and People's Amen should be in the same key and style. Many musical settings are available from such publishers as G.I.A. in Chicago and The Church Hymnal Corporation in New York. The *Worship Book* (The Upper Room) and *Songs for a Gospel People* (Wood Lake Books) are also important resources.

85

6) The Oblation (Offering): This is an explicit statement indicating that we offer our lives as a sacrifice of praise in the same way that Christ offered his own body for us. We commit our lives to the way of suffering and service that Jesus took.

This element of offering, following closely on the anamnesis, was present in Hippolytus's early prayer ("Remembering therefore his death and resurrection, we offer you this bread and cup..."). The once-and-for-all character of Jesus' sacrifice was lost by the medieval church which understood the mass to be a repeated sacrifice and assumed the power of forgiving sin. The Protestant Reformers removed all reference to sacrifice from the prayer. In *The Book of Common Order*, 1932, the United Church recovered the offering in the form of a self-offering: "...and here we offer and present unto thee, O Lord, ourselves, our souls and bodies, to be a reasonable, holy, and living sacrifice unto thee", a formula that Cranmer had relegated to the post-communion prayer in the 1552 *Book of Common Prayer*. Most contemporary prayers hold sacrifice in tension with thanksgiving in recognition that participation in God's saving purposes calls for the thankful giving of our very lives in response to God's self-giving.

7) Epiclesis: The word "epiclesis" is Greek, meaning a "calling upon" or a "calling to here". It refers to calling upon the Holy Spirit to come upon us and the gifts of bread and wine (e.g. "Loving God, pour out your holy Spirit upon us and upon these gifts, that they may be for us the body and blood of our Saviour, Jesus Christ." (*A Sunday Liturgy*, p. 18.). The activity of the Spirit in coming upon us and our gifts are a sign to us of the coming reign of Christ. The invocation of the Spirit heightens our expectations of the future and helps to keep us from being satisfied with the way things are in the present. The presence of Christ, through the action of the Holy Spirit, blesses our offering of ourselves to a new way of living

in the world. We become strengthened members of Christ's body working to bring about God's will of justice, mercy and peace for the world.

The Eastern church had an epiclesis as early as the fourth century. The Roman church, on the other hand, had no formal epiclesis, but merely requested that God bless the gifts without a specific reference to the Holy Spirit. In the East the epiclesis was regarded as the "moment of consecration" in contrast to the Institution Narrative, as in the West. The United Church *Book of Common Order* recovered the epiclesis via the Church of Scotland. (See: W.D. Maxwell, *An Outline of Christian Worship*, Oxford, 1936, pp. 160-162.) All modern prayers of great thanksgiving contain an epiclesis.

Supplications or Intercessions may follow, as a request for the benefits of the epiclesis (see Prayers I, II, IV and V in *A Sunday Liturgy*). The practice may have originated with the ancient Jewish prayer of blessing, which included requests that God would continue to look favourably upon Israel. In the medieval Roman church, with the falling away of the Prayers of the People, this was the only place in the service in which there were intercessions. Abuses connected with the selling of indulgences and masses for the dead led the Protestant Reformers to remove all intercessions from this prayer. When modern prayers include the option of brief intercessions, these are not a substitute for the Prayers of the People.

8) The Doxology: The earliest written ending of this prayer by Hippolytus of Rome included the doxology (words of praise), "...through your child Jesus Christ, through whom be glory and honour to you, to the Father and the Son with the Holy Spirit, in your holy church, both now and to the age of ages." Whatever doxology is used, it encapsulates the Trinitarian form of the whole prayer.

87

9) The People's Amen: To the doxology and the entire prayer the people respond AMEN (meaning, "So be it"). The Amen was a congregational response of assent and confirmation in the ancient synagogue service and Jesus frequently used it in the New Testament as an affirmation that what he said was true (often translated "verily" or "truly"). The early Christians continued the practice, as Paul indicates in I Cor. 14:16 when speaking of the Amen of the congregation at the thanksgiving. As Justin wrote around 150, "When the prayer of thanksgiving is ended, all the people present give their assent with an Amen." (I Apologia 65:3) It is only recent ecumenical practice that has restored to the people the opportunity of saying their own Amen. This response on the part of the people may be repeated or augmented by the choir. Any one of a number of musical settings of the Amen may be sung. Since this is a high point in the prayer a rousing Amen is appropriate.

This Amen at the conclusion of the prayer is parallel to the people's affirmation at the beginning in the Opening Dialogue. It ends the prayer on the note of praise with which it was begun. We again affirm what has been said on our behalf by the presider. More than an affirmation, however, the Amen is also a profession of faith. We join with Jesus, who is himself the "amen" (Rev. 3:14) and the response to all that God has done.

LORD'S PRAYER

This prayer immediately follows the prayer of Great Thanksgiving on communion Sundays or a Prayer of Thanksgiving on those Sundays not celebrating communion. The prayer may be understood to be asking not only for our physical bread, but also for the eucharistic bread of spiritual

88

sustenance. By the fourth century the Lord's Prayer had been attached to the prayer of Great Thanksgiving, following the Amen, perhaps because of the similarity of its themes of bread, forgiveness and peace. The Protestant Reformers followed the Eastern church in adding a positive note to Jesus' final words ("deliver us from evil") by preserving the ancient doxology first added by some early churches ("For the kingdom, the power, and the glory are yours, now and forever.") The Roman Church recently has also added this doxology to the liturgy. Translations of the Lord's Prayer have varied. A new translation has been produced which has been accepted by many denominations and is published in *A Sunday Liturgy*. Frequently the Lord's Prayer has been sung in the United Church. There are many musical settings for both the King James and modern versions.

ACTIONS AND GESTURES OF THE GREAT THANKSGIVING

The Great Thanksgiving is an action that is intended to engage all of the people. It can be argued that this is not a prayer of private devotion. Rather than bowing heads or following a printed version of the complete prayer in the bulletin, the people may participate more fully if they direct their attention toward Christ's Table. The presider stands immediately behind the Table, facing the people and in full view of all, leading them through the prayer.

Within the action of the Great Thanksgiving, there can be specific actions, responses and acclamations of the people. In ancient practice now being recovered, the people may stand for the prayer as an act of praise. The presider may use specific gestures to help lead people through the prayer and provide visual cues for their roles. (See illustrations in the Appendix.)

89

Simple traditional gestures can add beauty, grace and interest. Gestures become more important when the people have an active role in this prayer.

For instance, the presider may use the classical prayer posture known as the *orantes* during his or her portions of the prayer. When the *orantes* posture is used, the arms are extended and elbows bent in a comfortable manner from the body, with fingers relaxed and palms open and facing upward. When it is the people's turn to speak the presider may simply fold his or her hands at mid-chest level. The stance of praying with uplifted hands is referred to in many places in the Bible, for instance in the Psalms (28:2; 44:20; 63:4; 68:31; and 143:6) and in I Timothy 2:8, "I desire then that in every place [people] should pray, lifting holy hands without anger or quarreling." If desired, the people also could use the *orantes* posture for their parts, as art from the third to fifth centuries indicates they once did. During the Words of Institution, at "took bread" and "took the cup", the presider, having brought both hands to the rest position, may reach out with one or both hands to touch the bread and wine in a designating gesture, or else lift them to show the congregation. The bread remains unbroken and the wine unpoured, however, until the Fraction. Another possibility is to designate the elements here and to elevate them at the close of the prayer before the Amen.

The presider's hands need to be free if gestures are to be used during the Prayer. For this purpose the book that contains the prayer may rest flat or on a small stand or cushion on the Table, rather than being held in the presider's hands. A ceremonial book with an attractive cover and print large enough to be seen is of assistance here and may be made by the congregation, possibly to include art work of the children, prayers composed by the congregation, etc.

BREAKING OF THE BREAD (FRACTION)
AND POURING OF THE WINE

This action by the presider corresponds to the third of Jesus's four-part action in the Upper Room: "took", "gave thanks", *"broke"* and "gave". It has the practical purpose of preparing the elements for the communion. It also has a strong symbolic connection with Christ's body being broken and his blood being shed.

The Fraction had been placed at the Words of Institution in the *Book of Common Prayer*, 1662. The United Church's *The Book of Common Order* in 1932 offered a number of possibilities: "The 'Breaking' may stand alone, or be joined with the Prayer (gave thanks), or with the Delivery (gave)." (p. vi) It followed the Presbyterian practice in recovering the possibility of the Fraction as a distinct action in itself, immediately before the Communion and linked to the sharing of the elements, instead of during the great prayer. This location of the Fraction has been affirmed by other denominations more recently. The wine may also be poured into the chalice from a pitcher at this point, further to symbolize the readying of the meal and the shedding of Christ's blood. The pouring of the wine is best if it is seen and not hidden from view by the rims of the chalice and pitcher.

The actions of breaking the bread and pouring the wine may take place in silence or with accompanying words (i.e. "The body of Christ, broken for you..... The blood of Christ, poured out for you.") When there is no pouring of wine, the cup may simply be elevated. Just as words in a service need to be spoken loud enough for all to hear, it is important that the actions be seen clearly by all. If there are additional preparations that need to take place at this time, the elders will have designated who shall assist with these. For instance, an additional server or servers may be needed to come forward from the congregation to continue with the presider the preparations for sharing. Their cue to come forward may be the chalice being placed back on the Table following the pouring of the wine.

Depending upon how communion is to be served, there may be a need for additional vessels. These can be placed on a side table (credence table) before the service and moved to the Table by the servers at this point. The bread may be broken in preparation for distribution and placed into baskets (also brought from the side table at this time) for distribution. Another possiblity would be to have the loaf further broken when the people come forward to receive. If a common cup is to be used, napkins may be needed to wipe the rim of the cup(s). If additional chalices are needed, these may now be poured.

The time immediately before communion is commonly understood to be one of reverence and anticipation of the special meal about to be shared. Silence may be kept or instrumental music may be played or choral music sung. The *Agnus Dei* is an ancient fraction hymn. The presider and all of those serving may eat and drink now, as part of the preparation for serving. Their action will stand as a model for the rest of the congregation.

Once the servers have been given their assigned portions for serving and everything is ready, the presider may *invite* the people to communion with words such as, "The gifts of God for the People of God," and/or, "Come for all things are now ready." (Luke 14:17). This Invitation to communion, as found in *A Sunday Liturgy*, replaces the lengthier one that commonly introduced the Lord's Supper.

92

SHARING OF THE BREAD
AND CUP – COMMUNION

The climax of the whole service occurs when we are united to the living Christ and to the entire communion of saints, the whole company of believers on earth and in heaven, past, present and future.

Sharing of the bread and cup corresponds to the fourth of Jesus' Upper Room actions: "took", "gave thanks", "broke" and "*gave*". The word "communion" is a translation of the Greek *koinonia* meaning "partaking" or "sharing" in the body and blood of Christ. St. Paul used it in I Cor. 10:16 to denote a deep sense of unity between the communicants and Christ. The Protestant Reformers favoured the word "communion" for the whole service in order to emphasize the communal nature which they felt had been lost. The "thanksgiving" dimension of the word "eucharist" has only recently been recovered. In some churches the word "eucharist" is now used for the entire rite, and the word "communion" is used for the actual sharing of the bread and cup. The bread is our communion in the body of Christ and the wine is our communion in the blood of Christ.

POSTURE: Several postures are associated with communion. The 1969 *Service Book* said: "The people may remain in the pews, the elders carrying the bread and wine to them; the people may go forward and receive kneeling, or standing, at the chancel steps; or the people may gather in a group around the Table." (p. 1) In the Roman, Anglican and Methodist communions, the people have come forward to receive the elements at a balustrade or communion rail at the front of the sanctuary. In the Eastern churches, 1) *coming forward and standing* has been traditional. The church Fathers saw standing as the posture of a child approaching a parent, as a symbol

93

of resurrection, and as a recollection of the Passover command to eat in haste so as to be ready to depart on the Lord's business. (See: Hatchett, *Commentary on the American Prayer Book*, Seabury, 1981, p. 383.) In the West the custom of 2) *kneeling* for communion developed in the Middle Ages with the emphasis on the sacrament as an object of devotion and adoration. Some Reformed congregations (i.e. Protestant) in France, Alsace and Switzerland have standing as a norm. But most followed the Reformer Zwingli in adopting the practice of 3) *sitting* as a way of recovering as closely as possible the atmosphere of the meal in the Upper Room. Still today some Presbyterians in Holland and Westphalia continue the practice begun in Scotland of leaving their seats at the appropriate time of the service to sit around a table that is set up in the sanctuary or nave. Only under the influence of the English Puritans (Congregationalists), did the Scots adopt the practice of receiving in the pews. Some Methodists received communion in the pew. The practice of standing for communion is now being recovered by many denominations as a posture appropriate to an act of praise.

METHODS OF PARTAKING – INTINCTION: There are various methods of partaking of the elements. The early church used a common cup. With intinction the bread is dipped in the wine and the two are taken at the same time. This custom emerged in the 600s, when the bread and wine were placed directly on the tongue, possibly as a prevention against the sacrament being carried away from the church for superstitious purposes. It is still the preferred method of the Orthodox or Eastern Church and for hygienic reasons is often administered using a spoon containing the bread sprinkled with wine. Now permitted, intinction was banned by the Roman church in the thirteenth century and the people were allowed to partake of bread only.

SEPARATE CUPS: The Protestant Reformers argued that only communion in both bread and wine had scriptural warrant. The practice of using separate small glasses emerged at the end of the nineteenth century in Protestant churches for hygienic reasons. At the same time grape juice came to be used instead of wine. Ecumenical discussions are ongoing but tend to favour the return to a common cup for the symbolism of unity it provides. For hygienic reasons some are opting for intinction using a common cup. Currently in the United Church the most frequent way of receiving communion is in the pews with small individual cups.

WINE AND A LOAF OF BREAD: Whether to use wine or unfermented grape juice is a controversial issue in our church, which has had a history of support for the temperance movement. This stance has relaxed somewhat in recent years. Most of our churches do not use wine but some are beginning to affirm its rich symbolism. Prior to the 1870s and the invention of unfermented grape juice, wine was used.

More of our churches are moving toward the rich symbolism of a loaf of bread, however, instead of small cubes of decrusted sliced bread. One loaf can signify, when we partake of it, that we are one body, the body of Christ. Some use a loaf to retain the symbolic significance of the Fraction of the one loaf but distribute cubes. It may be preferable to have the bread broken into small pieces rather than cut in cubes, even if plates of bread are prepared in advance.

WORDS THAT ACCOMPANY THE DISTRIBUTION: If individuals partake of the elements as soon as they receive them, the presider, before the distribution of the bread, will say such words as, "This is the body of Christ broken for you," and will do likewise before the wine is distributed, "This is the blood of Christ shed for you." The words of the presider (and servers) may vary, as suggested in our service

95

books. When they are addressed to the whole congregation who are receiving in the pews they may be more elaborate.

Serving bread:

The Body of our Lord Jesus Christ, which was given for thee, preserve thee unto everlasting life. Take and eat this in remembrance that Christ died for thee, and feed on him in thy heart by faith with thanksgiving. (1932 & 1969)

or:

Take, eat; this is the Body of Christ which is broken for you; do this in remembrance of him. (1932 & 1969)

or:

The body of our Lord Jesus Christ keep you unto eternal life. (1969, blue, p. 12)

or:

Jesus Christ, the bread of life. (1969, blue, p. 20)

or:

The body of Christ, (given for you). (1984)

or:

The body of Christ, the bread of heaven. (1984)

Serving wine: The Blood of our Lord Jesus Christ, which was shed for thee, preserve thee unto everlasting life. Drink this in remembrance that Christ's Blood was shed for thee, and be thankful. (1932 & 1969) or:

This Cup is the New Covenant in the Blood of Christ, which is shed for the remission of the sins of many; drink ye all of it. (1932 & 1969)

or:

The blood of our Lord Jesus Christ keep you unto eternal life. (1969, blue, p. 12)

or:

Jesus Christ, the true vine. (1969, blue, p. 20)

or:

The blood of Christ, (shed for you). (1984)

or:

The blood of Christ, the cup of salvation. (1984)

RECEIVING IN THE PEWS – WAITING OR NOT WAITING TO PARTAKE: Our practices have varied. Individuals were often encouraged to partake immediately, as soon as they received the elements, the presider having already said such words as, "The body of Christ, given for you."

Alternatively, they were to wait until everyone had received. The serving elders, having distributed the bread or wine, would retake their seats and be served by the presider and/or those assisting the presider. The presider would then say words such as, "This is the body of Christ, given for you," and all would eat or drink together.

The practice of waiting for all to be served, instead of eating when the elements are received, originated in some Reformed and Free churches because it was thought to signify greater community with one another, since at a meal people customarily start together. Dr. George Pidgeon, the first moderator of the United Church, used this method of communion at the inaugural service of the United Church of Canada in 1925, possibly out of a desire to emphasize the equality of the uniting denominations. One contemporary criticism of this practice has been that it may suggest uniformity rather than genuine community in which individuals have the freedom to act when they are ready.

When communion is served in the pews it is preferable to have the people say the words of administration to each other ("The Body of Christ..."; "The Blood of Christ") as the bread and wine are given from one to another. Where these words are only said once by the presider before the bread and wine are distributed, there is a loss of connection between word and action and hence a loss of sacramental significance. As St. Augustine once said, "The word comes to the element and then you have a sacrament."

COMING FORWARD FOR COMMUNION: This method of receiving communion may have been experienced at an ordination/ commissioning, a confirmation, or at a special service such as Christmas Eve or Maundy Thursday, if not at the regular communion services of some of our churches. It has been the customary practice of Methodists, Lutherans, Anglicans, Orthodox and Roman Catholics. It is being recovered by other denominations in part because it is interpreted to make a clear statement of commitment on the part of the communicant and because it enacts the gathering of the community around Christ's Table.

This method of serving communion may occur as follows. (See illustration.) The people come forward down the centre aisle, proceed to vacant bread and wine "stations", and return down a side aisle. (In small churches without side aisles, the people may come forward and return using centre aisle.) Those not wishing or unable to come forward are offered the

98

elements in the pews by servers appointed to this task. Ushers ensure the ease of movement of the congregation. The people proceed first to receive the bread. As bread is placed by the server in each person's hand, words are spoken such as, "The Body of Christ broken for you," or "Jesus Christ, the bread of life." When the individual's name is known, it may be said. To these words each person responds with assent by saying, "Amen". The individual may then consume the bread (not all of it has to be consumed immediately – some may be taken back to the seat) and proceed to the adjacent station to receive the wine, again saying "Amen" after the appropriate words (i.e. "The blood of Christ shed for you," or "Jesus Christ the true vine"). The wine is then consumed and the individual returns to the pew. If wine is being used it need only touch the lips. If the individual is receiving by Intinction, she or he may retain the bread after receiving it and proceed to the wine station where she or he dips it into the cup before consuming it. When all have received, the servers at each station return the elements to the Table without ceremony and return to their seats.

Large or small numbers can be served quickly in a reverent yet unhurried atmosphere. For this to happen there must be sufficient stations of bread and wine; sufficient space at the front of the pews for there to be easy movement of the people to and from stations; and sufficient education and instruction of the congregation about both meaning and movement. As wine takes longer to serve, it is helpful, with large numbers, to have twice as many wine servers as bread servers.

Serving in this manner can significantly reduce the time we have traditionally taken to serve communion in our churches and may enable us to celebrate it more frequently, should we choose to do so. If a presider is sensitive to the question of time, a communion service may take place within the usual time allotted for worship.

ANOTHER METHOD FOR COMING FORWARD: A method that works best with smaller numbers is for the people to form a curved line around the front of the Table. Servers bring bread and wine to them, starting at the outer edge of the curve and moving toward the centre. This works with a minimum amount of delay and regimentation if the people leave as soon as they have received while others take their place without prompting. In larger gatherings this method takes more time than the stational approach.

SILENCE AND MUSIC: During communion silence may be maintained, for instance during Lent or Advent. Alternatively, instrumentalists may play, the choir may sing a communion anthem or the congregation may sing hymns of praise, communion and thanksgiving. This music is joyful and captures the intimacy of our union to Christ and to each other.

Singing may be facilitated by printing in the bulletin words such as, "During Communion the congregation is invited to join with the choir in the singing of hymns #332, #347, and #109." Even reading the hymn texts can be a catalyst to prayer. Another type of congregational singing today comes from the international ecumenical community at Taize, France. This uses a style in which the congregation sings a refrain (*ostinato*), either at the same time or alternating with a soloist (cantor) or choir. An excellent example of this is "Eat This Bread" in *The Music of Taize* (Vol. II, G.I.A. Publishers). Children easily can participate, either as singers or instrumentalists.

AFTER COMMUNION: Whatever method of administration is followed, when all have received communion, the Table is put in order prior to the closing prayer.

After the service is over the servers may take bread and wine to those unable to be present because of illness, imprisonment, etc. There is a service entitled "Communion to the Sick and Homebound" in *A Sunday Liturgy* (pp 38-39) which is designed to be led by an elder or other appointed lay person. A service like this is not a celebration of the sacrament, in its own right, but rather is an *extension* of that which has already been celebrated by the gathered community. It extends the number gathered around the Table and is an important means of involving members in the pastoral care of the church. Bread and wine that is not needed for this purpose may be consumed by members of the congregation following the service or disposed of in a respectful manner. One possibility is to give the bread to the birds and to pour the wine into the earth.

Our ways of celebrating communion are deeply rooted and valued. Festive occasions such as Christmas Eve provide opportunities for alternative modes such as coming forward to receive. If children are included in communion, as happens now in many United Churches, there is an incentive to seek new and more engaging ways of participating. With further experience we may learn as yet undiscovered ways of expressing in our actions the fullness of the meaning of the sacrament. But innovation in worship needs to provide not only new opportunities for faith expression but also a means for people to know that old ways are not gone forever. Our communion practices should take into account the varieties of people we have in our churches, allowing for a variety of practices, and not legislating one practice to the exclusion of all others.

PRAYER AFTER COMMUNION

This prayer is one of praise and commitment said by the presider or in unison by all. It ends the Service of the Table in gratitude for the strength we have received and turns us toward our tasks as members of Christ's body in the world.

Prior to the fifth century the eucharist ended with communion and a possible dismissal by the deacon. The post-communion prayer gradually emerged to provide a more formal conclusion. The United Church has had a post communion prayer from its beginning.

SENDING FORTH

Along with the post-communion prayer, other rites emerged as a way of concluding the entire service. Here we are reminded of God's blessing on us and of our scriptural commissioning to go into the world to love and serve the Lord. Underlying these is the understanding that we identify with the suffering of the world and that our worship continues as we put our faith to work.

This section, which is brief and to the point, *follows the post-communion prayer or, when the Eucharist is not celebrated, follows the Prayer of Thanksgiving and the Lord's Prayer.* It may usually occur in the order of a Hymn, Blessing and Sending Forth (Commissioning). Announcements may be given here, if they have not been placed elsewhere, as a sign of the people's life and work in the world. The section went without name in 1932 and 1969 and was given the current name in 1984 in *A Sunday Liturgy.* It focuses on our mission to the world as we depart from worship.

The HYMN is an affirmation of the people's commission to be the church in the world. It may be a recessional hymn for the worship leaders and the choir, coming after the Sending Forth, especially on special festive occasions. At Pentecost the entire congregation might process out of the sanctuary onto the lawn in a manner symbolic of the church going out into the world. During penitential seasons such as Advent or Lent, silence may at times be more appropriate than use of a final hymn.

The BLESSING or BENEDICTION is a declaration of God's favour upon the gathered community. It is said by the presider from the front, facing the people, with both arms raised and extended outward and palms turned slightly downward. (See illustration.) The practice of such a general blessing

103

emerged in the church when the majority of people were leaving having not received communion.

The SENDING FORTH or COMMISSIONING, which may be led by the presider, by a diaconal minister, or other leader may use these words: "Go forth in the name of Christ," or "Go in peace to love and serve the Lord." To this the people may respond, "Thanks be to God." This could be set to music if desired or other commissionings already set to music could be used. It has been customary in the United Church for the commissioning to precede the benediction as a ringing declaration of the people's call to be the church in the world. This simpler formula is based on the assumption that the whole service has been an act of commissioning and now all that is required at the conclusion is a dismissal of the people.

The POSTLUDE is not a formal part of the service in most congregations. Some listen to it while others begin conversations and hear it only as background. When a postlude does take place the congregation could be encouraged in the bulletin or by the choir to remain seated to listen. Another possibility is to offer a mini-recital following the service for those wishing to stay. This time could be used as a teaching time about music or other matters as well.

CHAPTER 5

Appendix

ACOUSTICS: One of the causes of unenthusiastic congregational participation, both spoken and sung, can be poor church acoustics. Some of our worship spaces may show our affluence and fail to provide good sound. We may have carpeted over hardwood floors, padded the pews, installed sound absorbing tile, and then may have found that we need to purchase expensive sound systems. Hospitals often use carpet and other sound absorbing material to isolate people, and that also can happen in well-padded churches. Sound-absorbing material can rob "spirit" from the worship. Individuals who cannot hear their neighbours sing, may themselves "hold back". In the theatre, the stage floors are left uncovered to project sound. In most churches acoustics would improve considerably if the carpeting were removed. Some of the need for sound systems would be removed and congregational participation would improve. (See: Scott R. Riedel, *Acoustics in the Worship Space*, Concordia, 1986)

BULLETIN: The bulletin assists with the worship but ideally demands minimal attention and allows eyes to be directed to the worship leaders. The bulletin can be one way of welcoming the visitors to the worship and ensuring they feel comfortable with the order and parts of the service. In addition to the

105

service itself, the bulletin might contain announcements, a congregational newsletter, records of congregational activities, forms to fill out for prayer requests, naming the sick, or requesting a visit. It may also on its cover offer an opportunity for reproducing art work by gifted members of the congregation. Space might also be provided for young children to colour, perhaps something related to one of the lessons.

It may not be necessary to print the service of worship in full. Most churches spend a great deal of energy and time to ensure that the bulletin is carefully prepared and that it adds to the worship experience. The bulletin is needed for unison portions of the service, congregational responses, announcing hymn numbers and the order of the service. In prayers involving a response, particularly prayers of Great Thanksgiving, simply the last line or two before the response need printing.

CHILDREN IN WORSHIP: Worship on Sunday is a gathering of the Christian community. When some are excluded, rich or poor, male or female, old or young, Christ's Body is diminished. Document currently under review in our church (including *Baptism and Renewal of Baptismal Faith*) are moving to reunify the rites of baptism, confirmation and first communion. The implication of these is that children, with their parents' consent, may be admitted to the Lord's Supper on the basis of their baptism.

Sacraments may be understood as gestures. There is a good argument that the "gestures" of worship, like the gestures of affection and of eating together in the home, should be a part of the primary experience of children. By these experiences children come to know who they are. Jesus said, "Let the little children come unto me."

One of the special gifts children contribute to worship is their wide-eyed expectancy and delight in surprise. For many of us the "celestial light" glimpsed in childhood has all too often, as Wordsworth said, "faded into the light of common day" ("Ode on Intimations of Immortality").

If children are to be present throughout the service, worship may need to be more engaging of all of the senses. This can be done without diminishing the cognitive or informational or educational aspect of worship. A sermon, for instance, may be written for the senses and incorporate the cognitive. It may be created to capture different listeners at different times. Metaphors and stories (including stories about children's experiences) appeal as much to children as to adults. The involvement of children in reading scripture, taking up the offering, singing and various kinds of symbolic movement (e.g. lighting a candle, carrying a banner or the Bible), can engage all of the children present. It also prepares children for the leadership roles they will have to assume in the church later in life.

CHOIR: The primary purpose of the choir is to provide leadership that enables the participation of the congregation in their sung or spoken parts of the service and in the hearing of God's Word. In addition a choir may make a musical offering that is beyond the capability of the congregation and that contributes to the hearing of the Word through praise and prayer. No anthem, motet or choral response will add to worship if it is not well-prepared, if it contradicts the mood and spirit of the worship, or if it is beyond the ability of the choir.

CHOIR LOCATION: The placement of the choir is more connected with the ear than it is with the eye. In most United Churches we are accustomed to the choir, in addition to its musical tasks, leading the congregation in standing or sitting. However, this can easily and appropriately be performed by the presider. The choir is best located where it is heard the best. Churches designing or redesigning their worship space would be wise to place the choir and organ in that spot from

107

which the sound is carried most effectively into the entire room. Expert advice is necessary for such testing. The congregation may appropriately direct its attention during worship to the Christian symbols (e.g. Pulpit, Table, Baptismal Font, Cross, stained glass, etc.) and to the leaders. When the choir is located at the front, care must be taken that the choir leader's actions do not draw undue attention. A primary purpose of the choir is to enable us better to hear the Word.

COLOUR IN WORSHIP: The colours of the sanctuary can contribute to the celebration of praise and thanksgiving by children and adults alike. The Christian year and the biblical story of salvation may be celebrated in the changing colours of the church year, for instance with the preaching stoles, the pulpit and table hangings (antependia), and banners.

The colours that are normally associated with grief or penitence are sombre colours. Bright colours we associate with hope and joy. When these colours become identified with certain times and seasons they help us to respond to portions of the Christian story then being highlighted.

The booklet *Vestments and Colours*, prepared by the Working Unit on Worship and Liturgy, and the Canadian Church Calendar, put out in part by the United Church, may be consulted for the seasonal colours through the Christian year. They are listed here:

Advent – purple or blue

Christmas/Epiphany – white

Season after Epiphany – green

Lent – purple or grey

Good Friday – black (absence of colour)

Easter – white or gold

Day of Pentecost – red

Season after Pentecost – green.

Special occasions throughout the year such as baptisms, ordinations, marriages and funerals may be marked by the white or gold of Easter or the red of of Pentecost.

GOWNS / VESTMENTS: What is worn by the primary leaders of the worship should assist our worship focus and not distract us from the Word or draw attention to personal taste or status. It is appropriate that anyone having a continuing function in front of the assembly be specially dressed for the occasion. Appropriate vestments may enhance the worship by their symbolic and aesthetic value.

Vestments in the medieval church had become very elaborate. The Protestant Reformers rejected vestments as part of their cleansing of a liturgy overladen with symbolism. Instead they opted for another medieval costume (i.e. the black Geneva gown) worn with or without an academic hood. This garment worn mainly by clergy, academics, and lawyers has tended to distinguish clergy as more learned than the laity. As university education no longer necessarily means theological education, the way it once did, much of its original symbolic significance has been lost in our age. With the recovery of colour in worship, black (which is the absence of colour) is being seen as particularly appropriate for Good Friday.

A garment which is increasingly being adopted by many denominations including the United Church is the ALB. An alb is a long, loose-flowing, white or off-white gown. (*Alba* in Latin means white.) In the early church those who were newly baptized had placed on them a similar kind of garment as a symbol of forgiveness and the new life that is theirs in Christ. An alb might be worn by any baptized person when called upon to serve in a continuing function for a worship service. It is particularly appropriate for the diaconal minister and the presider. The mark of ordered ministries, however, is not the alb but the STOLE. Worn by the ordained, the stole is placed over the shoulders, around the neck and hanging down in front. Diaconal ministers may wear the stole over the left shoulder like a sash and tying or pinning it in place at the right hip. Members of the congregation who are not having a continuing function at the front, for instance those who are reading scripture, leading in prayers or serving communion, need not wear an alb. By wearing ordinary clothing and by coming forward and returning to their places in the congregation, they may symbolize their coming forth from the congregation.

HYMN SINGING: It is generally accepted that hymn singing has declined in the modern Protestant church. The difficulty of many musical settings in the **Hymn Book** is one of the popular reasons, but there are others. These include: 1) We do far less singing of hymns in the home. 2) We worship less frequently (and sometimes with less regularity!) than we once did. 3) We have created worship spaces with poor acoustics. 4) Insufficient attention has been given to the musical training of clergy and church musicians. 5) Our selection of hymns to be sung often has become "stale". 6) Our church schools for the most part are not teaching the great hymns. A case can be made for regarding every hymn in the hymnal as a children's hymn.

The leaders of most of the great spiritual movements in the church realized that if they were going to be successful the people had to sing the faith. They wrote hymns that told faith stories that fit the times. What people sang shaped their faith and their theology. We might improve our hymn-singing by singing more frequently, at board meetings, in the UCW (United Church Women), at church dinners, in rehearsal or informal hymn-singing times before church, and in the home. Members may be encouraged not only to read their Bibles but to include the contents of hymns in their routines of daily prayer.

HYMN SELECTION: Ideally this will be a task shared by a team like a Worship Committee including the minister(s) and musician. Hymn selection needs to take place in connection with the images and ideas in the scripture lessons. Those planning worship might engage in Bible study together on a regular basis. This can be assisted with the use of a Lectionary. Introduction of new hymns requires that time be planned for teaching the hymn to the congregation, possibly by the children in the Time for Children, or in a rehearsal or hymn-singing time before the service. Worship planners can keep abreast of new hymns by receiving such journals as *The Hymn*; *Reformed Liturgy and Music*; or *Reformed Worship*.

INCLUSIVE LANGUAGE: The purpose of inclusive language in worship is that all people might equally feel included in the worship of God. Where this does not happen, or where people experience negative imagery attached to themselves, they will probably not attend worship. Inclusive language extends beyond the matter of male-female imagery, around which there has been much controversy. It is concerned with using words that welcome people of all races and ethnic backgrounds, and people of all ages at various stages of maturity and physical and emotional ability. It is concerned with affirming the worth of people whatever their life experience may be, whether unemployed or employed; part of a nuclear family or not; single, married, separated or divorced; facing an illness or suffering an addiction; coping with some form of disability; or choosing to be known by their devotion to a particular cause or need.

Scriptural warrant for inclusive language tends to be found in a number of places including I Corinthians 8, where Paul cautions against our behaviour becoming a stumbling block to others, and in Galatians 3:28, which says, "There is neither Jew nor Greek, slave nor free, male nor female, for you are all one in Christ Jesus."

Within the last decade, the word "man" and male pronouns have ceased to be generic and no longer are generally understood to be inclusive of both male and female. They tend to make women invisible. This has been a painful issue in the church. Inclusive language does not need to be awkward or obvious. Use of inclusive language, for instance in most contemporary publications, is rarely noticeable. With regard to references to God, our goal in worship should be to draw more on the many female images of God in the Bible, as well as the male, so as to provide an appropriate balance.

Detailed suggestions for inclusive language may be found in the document approved by General Council, "Guidelines for Inclusive Language", and in, "The Words We Sing: An Inclusive Language Guide to the Hymn Book" (The Working Unit on Worship and Liturgy, Division of Mission in Canada, 1984).

LECTIONARY AND CALENDAR: Most of us who grew up in the church were accustomed to discovering the Sunday readings only when in the service. How these were chosen or why was not something we presumed to know. What they are affects the life of the individual congregation.

The United Church has always provided a set of lessons to be read in church through the year, but the use of these tables of lessons is optional. This is because we are part of what has been known as "the free pulpit tradition", which means that ministers have been given the option of choosing for themselves which lessons will be read and preached in a service. As the *Service Book* says, "This table [of lessons] is intended to be suggestive, not restrictive. When the calendar or local usage raise complications, or when circumstances suggest the use of other readings, the best criterion for selection will be the judgement of the minister." (p. 318, green; p. 255, blue)

In the last fifteen years a surprising development has taken place which has had enormous impact on our denomination. It is the adoption of a lectionary known as *The Common Lectionary* (Church Hymnal Corporation, NY, NY, 1983) by many in our order of ministry. In an earlier form this was known as the COCU (Consultation on Church Union) Lectionary, and now is often referred to as the "ecumenical lectionary" or simply the "lectionary". These names really refer to a number of denominational variations on the 1969 Roman Catholic Lectionary (a result of Vatican II), the value of which was immediately recognized by Protestants. It set before the congregations a wider range of scripture in a more systematic way than had previously been possible. In 1983, The Consultation on Common Texts, with United Church participation, produced the revised version now widely used.

"Lectionary" is a strange word for many. The word "lection" is another word for "scriptural lesson", derived from the Latin word meaning "a chosen reading". A "lectionary", therefore, is a list or book of scriptural lessons for use in worship. The lessons are provided according to the seasons of the Christian year.

The use of the lectionary can be traced back to the service in the ancient synagogue. It is not clear in Luke 4 whether Jesus was reading from the lectionary-prescribed reading or one that he had chosen for the occasion. The synagogue lectionary had fixed readings chosen from the scriptures for the Jewish feast days, and for the days in between there were continuous readings through biblical books chosen at local discretion.

The connection between the synagogue lectionary and one developed by the early Christians is uncertain. The early Christian lectionary centred on the major Christian feast days. One of the earliest prescribed readings was Exodus 12. This account of the deliverance from Egypt and Jewish passover was used to describe the great festival of redemption, the Christian Easter.

Throughout the history of the church there have been different kinds of lectionaries. There are Sunday lectionaries for the Sunday services, Festival Day lectionaries for special feast days, daily lectionaries for morning and evening prayer services, funeral and wedding lectionaries, and special occasion lectionaries as might be drawn up by a congregation in relation to an ongoing study project. Lectionaries further differ from each other on the period of time upon which they base their cycle of readings: Sunday lectionaries have commonly been anywhere from one to six year cycles.

The Book of Common Order of 1932 provided a one year lectionary. It was largely borrowed from the Anglican *Book of Common Prayer*, giving the collects or daily prayers with the readings. As was the practice from the sixth century, the readings for each Sunday were most commonly the epistle and the gospel, with only the occasional Old Testament passage. The gospel lesson was always to be read.

In using a lectionary the calendar becomes important. The readings need to match the dates and seasons in the Christian year. The pattern of the Christian year in the United Church today (with the exception of the 1969 *Service Book*) is essentially the same as in 1932:

Advent (the four weeks prior to Christmas in which we anticipate the coming of Christ, both in his birth and at the end of time – the beginning of the Christian year – traditionally penitential)

Christmas (God becoming flesh in the Incarnation) Dec. 25

Christmas Season Dec. 24 – Jan. 6

Epiphany (which means appearance or manifestation of God, traditionally focusing on such events as the descent of the Spirit at Jesus' baptism, on God's manifestation to the Gentiles, symbolized by the Magi, and on the first miracle of Jesus' ministry at Cana in turning water into wine) Jan. 6

Season after Epiphany

Lent (six weeks [40 days excluding Sundays] prior to Easter beginning with Ash Wednesday, originally a time of preparation for baptism at Easter – penitential)

Holy Week (Individual days before Easter – 1932.) From Palm/Passion through Maundy Thursday and Good Friday to Easter.

Ascension Day (40 days after Easter, marking Christ's ascent into heaven)

Palm/Passion Sunday (recent) [Sunday next before Easter – 1932] (The 1932 book reads, "from this day until Good Friday the eyes of the Church are fastened on the Cross of Our Lord" p. 85. – There are current attempts to recover Palm/Passion Sunday with the emphasis on Jesus' suffering and to move away from calling it simply Palm Sunday with the premature emphasis on joyful celebration. The service thus begins with the Palm Sunday reading of Jesus' triumphal entry into Jerusalem and proceeds during the service of the Word with the account of

Jesus' passion – his suffering and dying on the cross.)
Passion Sunday readings.

Easter Day (celebrating the resurrection of Christ from the dead) A moveable feast which always falls on the first Sunday after the first full moon after the Spring Equinox. Thus it falls anywhere between Mar. 22 and Ap. 25.

Easter Season (Easter Day until Pentecost)

Pentecost (meaning in Greek, "fiftieth", and marking the descent of the Spirit on the disciples seven weeks [fifty days] after Easter)

Season after Pentecost (continues until Advent)

Trinity Sunday [or the first Sunday after Pentecost]

To these seasons traditional Christian colours have now been applied (see: Appendix, *Colours).

The arrangement of the readings for the different seasons is explained at the beginning of the 1932 volume:

"The Lord's people should hear the great passages of Scripture at least once a year. The *Table of Lessons* has therefore been confined largely to those central passages that gather closely about: (1) Christ's work of Redemption (Advent to Pentecost, half the year), and (2) the application of that work to believers (Pentecost to Advent,the other half of the year.)". (p.v.)

The *Common Lectionary* has returned to this understanding and developed it further. As in 1932, the life of Jesus as recorded in the gospels is the focus of Advent to Easter, and the life and mission of the church is the focus to Christmas. The Epistle readings are chosen independent from the Gospel on

116

the basis of a continuous reading, week to week. It allows for continuous treatment of entire books of the Bible instead of jumping, as in 1932 and 1969, from one book to another week by week.

Like the Roman Catholic Lectionary on which it is based, the *Common Lectionary* devotes a year to each of the synoptic Gospels: Year A – Matthew; Year B – Mark; Year C – Luke. Synoptic means that they treat their material in a similar way with regard to form, content and statement. The Gospel of John, which is not one of the synoptics, is treated in each of the three years primarily in Lent, the Easter Season, and on additional Sundays particularly in the year devoted to Mark. While John has no single year devoted to it, roughly the same percentage of it is covered as Luke.

One important change *The Common Lectionary* has made over its Roman Catholic and other predecessors has been that Old Testament lessons are no longer chosen simply in light of the gospels. The criticism had been that the Old Testament was made to serve the New Testament, rather than standing on its own. Now, particularly in the Season after Pentecost, Old Testament books are also given continuous reading. The widespread popularity of the new lectionary means that in many churches, Roman Catholic, Protestant and Anglican, the same lessons are being read each Sunday. The Roman lectionary differs from the *Common Lectionary* in roughly one-fifth of its readings (some of these are because of a slightly different calendar or church year).

We may now turn to consider an innovative step of the United Church which went awry. It is the 1969 *Service Book* lectionary. The Church recognized that a revision of the one-year lectionary was overdue: broader scriptural readings and regular exposure to God's Word in the Old Testament was needed. To accomplish this, it published, in the back, a three-

117

year Table of Lessons with three possible readings for each Sunday. The intent was to offer "a means whereby over a three-year period the main themes of Scripture may be set before a congregation comprehensively and systematically." (p. 317, green; p. 254, blue) It was innovative in two ways. First, it used as its base revisions proposed by Dr. A.A. McArthur in his 1958 SCM publication, *The Christian Year and Lectionary Reform*. McArthur selected themes for each year on the basis of doctrine and arranged them in the logical progression he found in the Apostles' Creed. Second, the lectionary tried to "serve as a vehicle for teaching and preaching" (p. 317): the readings and the themes for each year arose out of the United Church's new Sunday School program called *The New Curriculum*. Year One focused on God's Purpose, Year Two on God's Way, and Year Three on God's People. The most marked feature of this calendar based on doctrine was a Season of creation which celebrated the first person of the Trinity.

The 1969 lectionary provided for a strong thematic approach to teaching and preaching and developed the important link between education and worship. One thing it did not do was allow for continued treatment of any one book of the Bible. In retrospect we might ask: Should doctrine and education dictate worship or should they follow from worship? The order in 1969 was backwards. Education comes out of liturgy and leads back to liturgy, not the other way around. It is worship that is at the centre of our experience together. Now that the *New Curriculum* is rarely used, the Table of Lessons is of diminished value.

The innovation of the United Church proved ill-timed because in the same year that it was published, the Roman Lectionary appeared and quickly found broad acceptance.

None of the new lectionaries based on the Roman Catholic Lectionary claims to be perfect. They are simply the best means now available for ensuring that in a three-year period congregations are exposed to most of the Bible. As a tool it need not be followed or followed rigidly. The reasons our church is using it, however, include: the exposure it gives to the scriptures; the availability of resources (the United Church worship and educational resource *Gathering* is lectionary-based); the benefits clergy are finding in cooperative preparation for Sundays; and, perhaps most important, the contribution to the musical and educational life of the church (i.e. Sunday School, Bible study, group projects) which can be planned in advance around the year's lessons.

A new grassroots United Church education curriculum based on the lectionary, called *The Whole People of God*, is being received enthusiastically by many congregations in the United Church.

PULPIT, TABLE AND FONT: If we walked into most United Churches we could expect either to find a pulpit near the centre of the chancel area or to find what is called a split chancel, with *both* a pulpit and a lectern. If there is only a pulpit, both the reading and the preaching occur there. If there is a lectern, it is used for the reading and the pulpit is used for the preaching.

In worship everything speaks. For instance, if the walls of the sanctuary are chipped and dirty or if the communion cloth is crisp and clean, something is said about our worship. We may never have questioned what we are saying by having both a pulpit and a lectern in a church. It is no wonder – they are not the easiest things to change! But perhaps for any new or proposed church building we might question what they say. It can be a positive thing to honour the past. But on the negative side, the practice of having both pulpit and lectern can create a division between the reading and the preaching. The Word of God read and the Word of God preached are one, but pulpit

119

and lectern can make them appear separate. When the sermon does not immediately follow the scripture reading the connection is further lost.

The practice of having both pulpit and lectern stems from the medieval practice of splitting the choir for antiphonal singing (singing alternately in response to each other). This was a common practice of the medieval monastic choir, particularly in the daily offices of morning and evening prayer. The two parts of the choir and their leaders faced each other from separate lecterns. From one of these was sung the Epistle and from the other the Gospel (this was during a period of Church history in which only two lessons were used). When there was preaching (often there was none), and when it was based on the scripture, it was based on the Gospel and was preached from the Gospel side of the chancel. Pulpits eventually became raised in part to make the preacher visible.

In the Reformed tradition, the higher pulpits came to emphasize the proclamation of the Word over other parts of the service. They also made a statement that the authority of the Word was above and beyond the level of the people. (Today we might instead understand its authority more with reference to its capacity to move people's minds and hearts.) Some preachers, in order to be in closer relationship to the people, are now leaving the pulpit to preach. Such a practice can also result in a loss of the symbolic connection between the read word and the preached word. Also, the congregation can be left with the distracting symbol of a pulpit that is empty during the sermon. It might be better for the preacher occasionally to move out from behind the pulpit but remain adjacent to it during the preaching or for the architecture of the church to be altered.

In reconceiving the chancel area, it is helpful to remember that all that is necessary is a lectern that can serve

120

as a pulpit and place of reading, a chair for the presider, the Table, and the baptismal Font. The lectern/pulpit should be constructed in such a way as to allow a full view of both the Bible and the reader and/or preacher. It should be placed in proximity to the people in order to express the character of the proclamation of the Word as God's personal word addressed to each of us.

The Protestant practice of referring to Christ's Table as a table rather than altar has implications for both its shape and its location in the church. The Table should look like a table rather than an altar or a tomb. In the Middle Ages altars were tomb-shaped because they actually were places of burial. We speak of a table because the sacrament of the Lord's Supper is a communion meal. The Table, like the pulpit/lectern, should be placed in proximity to the people rather than at the end of a long narrow chancel which suggests that God is not near. Because the action of communion is one of gathering at the Table, ideally there should be plenty of gathering space around and in front of the Table. The Table, placed in this way, expresses the hospitality and intimacy of the communion meal. These attributes are increasingly being used to refer to God's presence. The mystery of God's presence resides in the wonder that our great God can come so near, rather than in a sense of remoteness as is evoked by some traditional church buildings.

The two sacraments in our church are Baptism and Holy Communion. Like the Table, the Font should be clearly visible and occupy a prominent place in the sanctuary. It serves as a sign of the grace we have received and through which we are made members of Christ's body. Ideally the Font will be located in the chancel or, if the worship space is flexible and the congregation can easily move for baptisms, the Font can be located by the entrance to the sanctuary where it is a good symbol of our entry into faith. In this location it might be constructed as a fountain of running water that is a constant reminder of the water of our baptism. A fountain with a pool could also serve for other services such as foot washing.

WORSHIP COMMITTEES/ SESSION: In the United Church it is the Session or Unified Board which has responsibility for oversight of worship and use of the worship space. In some churches the session delegates a worship committee to act. In either case there are two general approaches to the oversight of worship. In some churches the professional staff make most of the decisions and the committee functions to approve or modify them, and may occasionally take a more active role in planning special services. In other churches the worship committee, in consultation with the professional staff, will plan and coordinate the worship, assist with the bulletin, recruit appropriate people to read or lead prayers, plan music, arrange art, rehearse those involved in the service, and link with the church groups to ensure that the various needs are being met. The responsibility for coordination of particular services with the Presider can be rotated, week by week, among the members. Some ministers may fear that their own oversight functions may be weakened by a strong worship committee and that rather than being an asset such a committee might create problems. If a worship committee is informed about worship practice, however, it can in fact be a great help in both the planning and the interpretation of worship for the congregation.

WORSHIP REFORM IN A CONGREGATION: Changes in local worship are not legislated but rather evolve out of a process of education, consultation, discussion and pastoral care. Worship is dear to our hearts and needs to be a community expression based in sound understanding, not one individual's decision based on personal preference. Many of our worship practices developed over many years, often without much congregational participation and sometimes without sound rationale.

How does a congregation participate more fully in both the planning and the conduct of worship? A key problem is that congregations cannot make decisions about worship they have not experienced. One approach that has proved effective is for the appropriate church committee or board to make worship a central focus of the congregation for a limited time, say a three to six-month period. Each Sunday one practice that is new to the congregation might be tried (i.e. congregational responses to the scripture reading). This will be highlighted in the Bulletin, in a brief rehearsal time before the service, and elsewhere with explanation of the history and meaning of the action. Each Sunday the practice from the week before is continued. Written responses are invited each week and worship committee members are specially identified with name tags in the coffee hour. In the final month of this education time the entire service, as envisioned, is followed in order to allow a sustained familiarity on the part of everyone.

At the end of this period a forum on worship might be held, perhaps with a guest trained in leading worship workshops. The purpose is to interpret what has happened, answer questions, and collect responses. It could then be left to the worship committee to make decisions and implement them.

PRESIDER'S GESTURES

fig. 1   *fig 2*
The Lord be with you.   The grace of Christ attend you

PRESIDER'S GESTURES
AT THE GREAT THANKSGIVING

fig. 1
orantes posture
while presider speaks

fig. 2
hands at rest
while people respond

fig. 3
Jesus took bread

Jesus took the cup
of wine

fig. 4
Through Christ,
with Christ and
in Christ

GATHERING FOR COMMUNION

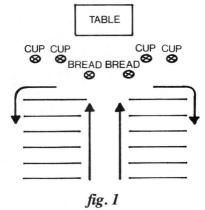

fig. 1
People coming forward to stations

A procession forms in the centre aisle and people receive at stations in front of the table moving to either side in order to return to their seats by the side aisles. The presider administers the bread and other servers the bread and/or wine. For larger numbers there may be two cup servers for every one bread server.

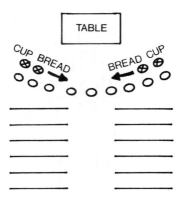

fig. 2
People gathering in table groups

The people come forward and form a curved line in front of the table. Servers bring the bread and wine to the people starting from the outer edge and moving toward the centre. Individuals may leave as soon as they have received leaving room for others to take their places. This approach is better in smaller gatherings.

126